IMPROVE YOUR READING: IMPROVE YOUR JOB

Basic Reading Skills for the Working Adult

Jeanne M. Miller

A FIFTY-MINUTE™ SERIES BOOK

CRISP PUBLICATIONS, INC.
Menlo Park, California

IMPROVE YOUR READING: IMPROVE YOUR JOB
Basic Reading Skills for the Working Adult

Jeanne M. Miller

CREDITS
Editor: **Nancy Shotwell**
Layout and Composition: **Interface Studio**
Illustration: **Ralph Mapson**
Cover Design: **Paine Communications, Inc.**

Copyright © 1991 by Crisp Publications, Inc.
Printed in the United States of America

English language Crisp books are distributed worldwide. Our major international distributors include:

CANADA: Reid Publishing Ltd., Box 69559—109 Thomas St., Oakville, Ontario, Canada L6J 7R4. TEL: (905) 842-4428, FAX: (905) 842-9327

Raincoast Books Distribution Ltd., 112 East 3rd Avenue, Vancouver, British Columbia, Canada V5T 1C8. TEL: (604) 873-6581, FAX: (604) 874-2711

AUSTRALIA: Career Builders, P.O. Box 1051, Springwood, Brisbane, Queensland, Australia 4127. TEL: 841-1061, FAX: 841-1580

NEW ZEALAND: Career Builders, P.O. Box 571, Manurewa, Auckland, New Zealand. TEL: 266-5276, FAX: 266-4152

JAPAN: Phoenix Associates Co., Mizuho Bldg. 2-12-2, Kami Osaki, Shinagawa-Ku, Tokyo 141, Japan. TEL: 3-443-7231, FAX: 3-443-7640

Selected Crisp titles are also available in other languages. Contact International Rights Manager Suzanne Kelly at (415) 323-6100 for more information.

Library of Congress Catalog Card Number 90-84075
Miller, Jeanne M.
Improve Your Reading: Improve Your Job
ISBN 1-56052-086-8

This book is printed on recyclable paper with soy ink.

TO THE READER...

In today's competitive marketplace, organizations wanting to increase productivity need workers who can read well. Reading well means grasping the intended meaning of written communications fast and accurately and using that understanding to solve on-the-job problems, improve the quality of work processes, and better serve customer needs.

Mastering one's reading skills is a gradual process. It doesn't happen automatically, but becomes reachable with the help of clear explanations, demonstrations, practice, and good coaching.

The purpose of *Improve Your Reading: Improve Your Job* is to serve as your active partner and coach in your process of becoming a better reader—and a more competent, promotable, and valued employee. It will help you identify your strengths, close educational gaps, sharpen skills you already have, and develop new ones necessary for your success in today's workplace.

SECTION I, WORK READING SKILLS, directs you to the types of communications you will meet most frequently in your daily work. SKILLS 3–7 show you how to locate and interpret the key information you need to perform your job well. **SECTION II, WORKING VOCABULARY**, provides lists of words and their meanings that will help you better understand some of the often confusing technical terms and jargon commonly used at work.

If you find you need practice in some of the basic elements or components of reading, **SECTION III, BACK-UP SKILLS**, will increase your confidence in recognizing words, pronouncing them correctly, learning word meanings and how to determine word meanings from word parts and surrounding text. This section also builds alphabetizing and dictionary skills.

Your investment of time and effort in upgrading your reading skills will give you a distinct advantage in your work and life. I'm confident it will make your job easier and more satisfying. It will enable you to better manage—and even enjoy— the business of life.

Jeanne Miller

Jeanne M. Miller

i

TO THE TRAINER...

WHO WILL BENEFIT FROM THIS BOOK

1. New readers/ESL (English as a Second Language) students

HOW TO USE THIS BOOK
(*Suggestions*)

With the planned direction and regular assistance of a reading instructor or tutor.

1. Begin with **SKILL 13**. This skill module uses the language-experience model to aid new readers in learning to recognize in print the words they use daily to perform their jobs. The model is developmental. *Gradually* integrate all the steps into instruction sessions.

2. Adults learn to read by reading materials that draw upon their life and work experiences. As the new readers develop their skills in reading print *they've dictated* and *you've recorded* for their study, select phonetic, word-building, and related skills from the **BACK-UP SKILLS** section of the book (SKILLS 13–22), beginning with SKILLS 14–19, to expand recognition of sound and syllable patterns to new contexts.

3. Continue with SKILLS 1 and 2.

4. Then SKILLS 3–12, in the order most appropriate to the individuals' present or target jobs.

2. Employees/Job-seekers preparing for GED testing

On a self-paced basis, or with the guidance and help of a classroom instructor/trainer. Individuals or groups may find it valuable to use the **BACK-UP SKILLS** section for review (focusing on SKILLS 16 and 20–22) before proceeding to the **WORK READING SKILLS** section. SKILLS 1, 2, 5, 6, and 7 will help prepare for standardized tests.

WHO WILL BENEFIT FROM THIS BOOK	HOW TO USE THIS BOOK *(Suggestions)*
3. Employed high school graduates whose reading skill levels need upgrading to match the requirements of their jobs	Same as above. If the "YOUR TURN!" exercises in the **BACK-UP SKILLS** section can be completed with ease, proceed to **WORK READING SKILLS.** Spend ample time working through and applying the model in SKILL 1 to workplace materials. Comprehension will improve significantly as readers learn these techniques for "managing" the reading process and experiment with them at repeated intervals. Practice applying the steps in SKILLS 2, 3, 5, and 6 to additional workplace materials.
4. Employed high school graduates preparing for college admission or technical education programs	On a self-paced basis, with occasional review/critique of completed exercises by a basic skills trainer/reading assistant.
5. Employees needing improvement —or a brush-up in specific areas of reading to increase their potential for career advancement	On an independent study basis, targeting the skills needed most. Use SKILLS 1–4 to increase comprehension, and SKILLS 12, and 20–22 (8 and 11, if appropriate) to build vocabulary.

SPECIAL FEATURES

* All material is tailored to employed adults or adults preparing for employment. Listed words have been carefully selected, considering adult needs as well as current organization structures and requirements.

* The strategies and techniques provided, along with the follow-through ("ON YOUR WAY") exercises, teach self-management of the reading process. They encourage users to take initiative and responsibility for developing skills and habits and continually applying them to their workplace reading.

* Instructors can supplement the skill modules with additional skillbuilding exercises and printed materials used regularly by the trainees in their jobs.

* Skills taught in one module are reinforced in others.

* Reference sections are provided for on-the-job use.

* The book can easily be converted into a training program. A typical course might run for 12 weeks, covering two skill modules a week, in two, 1–2 hour sessions. The instructor can rearrange the sequence of the modules to meet individual, group, or organization needs.

TABLE OF CONTENTS

SECTION

I

WORK READING SKILLS

SKILL 1: STEERING YOUR COURSE

Active Reading For Meaning

Who are you? You are an individual—one of a kind, an "original," as they say—with a unique set of experiences.

You've had interesting experiences—some good, some unpleasant, some exhilarating—but all weavers of the fabric of your individuality.

You've learned much in the course of growing, and your knowledge has enriched the lives of the people around you.

You've faced challenges, overcome difficult hurdles, and accomplished important tasks. In the process, you've acquired and developed skills to help yourself and others.

You have feelings that run deep and sometimes strong. You have opinions and values that shape your daily actions and reactions to what you see and hear.

In short, you bring a unique background and a wealth of experience to your workplace, your job, and your reading.

Reading has everything to do with who you are, because **reading is an interaction between you and a printed text.**

> Reading is the active, deliberate process of searching for meaning from text. You steer the course your reading will take!

Improving your reading requires:

- Knowing and valuing what you bring to the printed word.
- Learning how to use your knowledge and experience more effectively to meet your reading goals.
- Taking responsibility for your reading improvement.

Keeping in mind that your goal is to become a self-directed reader, approach each piece of reading this way:

STRATEGIES FOR BUILDING READING COMPREHENSION— A MODEL

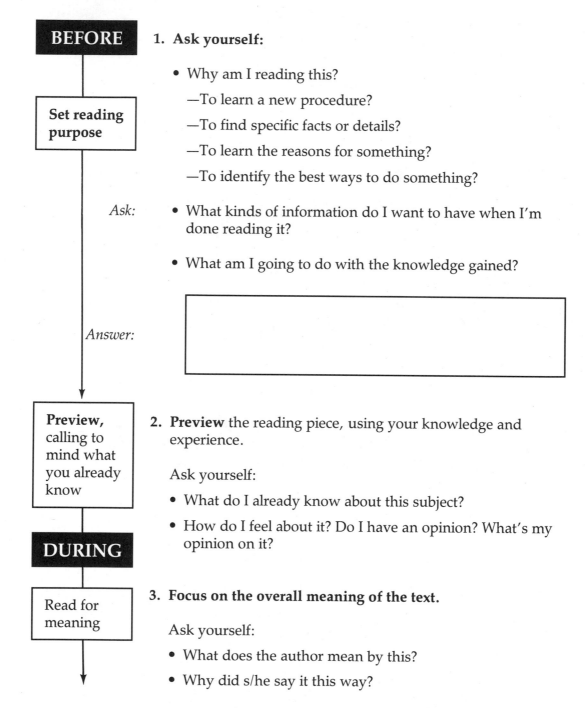

BEFORE

Set reading purpose

1. **Ask yourself:**

   - Why am I reading this?
     - —To learn a new procedure?
     - —To find specific facts or details?
     - —To learn the reasons for something?
     - —To identify the best ways to do something?

Ask:
   - What kinds of information do I want to have when I'm done reading it?

   - What am I going to do with the knowledge gained?

Answer:

Preview, calling to mind what you already know

2. **Preview** the reading piece, using your knowledge and experience.

   Ask yourself:
   - What do I already know about this subject?
   - How do I feel about it? Do I have an opinion? What's my opinion on it?

DURING

Read for meaning

3. **Focus on the overall meaning of the text.**

   Ask yourself:
   - What does the author mean by this?
   - Why did s/he say it this way?

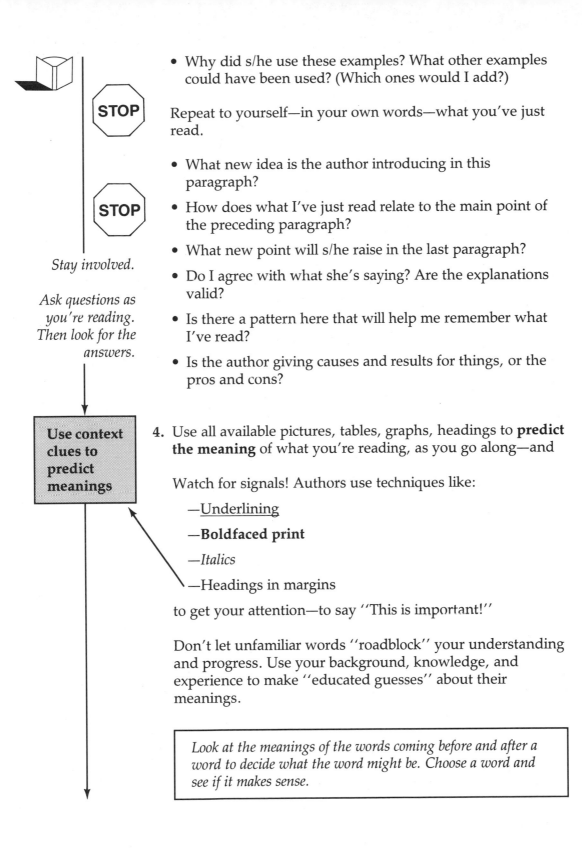

- Why did s/he use these examples? What other examples could have been used? (Which ones would I add?)

STOP

Repeat to yourself—in your own words—what you've just read.

STOP

- What new idea is the author introducing in this paragraph?
- How does what I've just read relate to the main point of the preceding paragraph?
- What new point will s/he raise in the last paragraph?
- Do I agree with what she's saying? Are the explanations valid?
- Is there a pattern here that will help me remember what I've read?
- Is the author giving causes and results for things, or the pros and cons?

Stay involved.

Ask questions as you're reading. Then look for the answers.

Use context clues to predict meanings

4. Use all available pictures, tables, graphs, headings to **predict the meaning** of what you're reading, as you go along—and

Watch for signals! Authors use techniques like:

—<u>Underlining</u>

—**Boldfaced print**

—*Italics*

—Headings in margins

to get your attention—to say "This is important!"

Don't let unfamiliar words "roadblock" your understanding and progress. Use your background, knowledge, and experience to make "educated guesses" about their meanings.

> *Look at the meanings of the words coming before and after a word to decide what the word might be. Choose a word and see if it makes sense.*

(continued next page)

STRATEGIES: A MODEL (Continued)

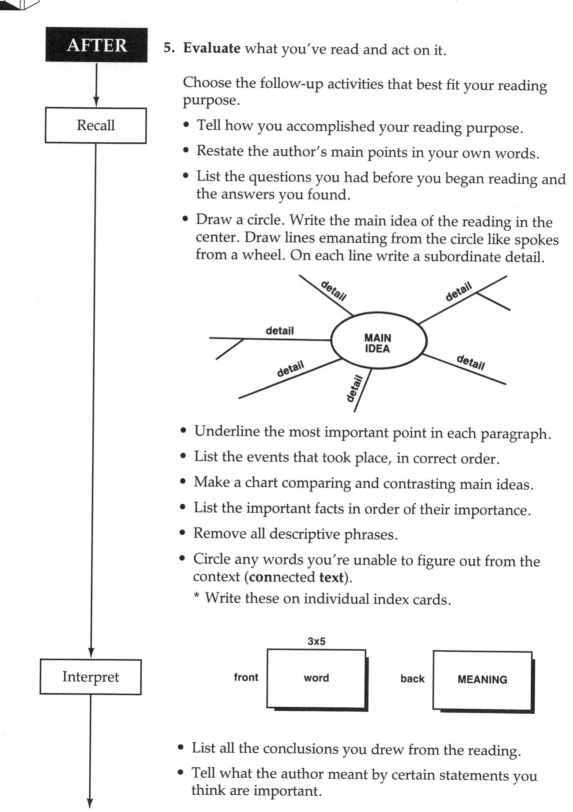

AFTER

Recall

5. Evaluate what you've read and act on it.

Choose the follow-up activities that best fit your reading purpose.

- Tell how you accomplished your reading purpose.

- Restate the author's main points in your own words.

- List the questions you had before you began reading and the answers you found.

- Draw a circle. Write the main idea of the reading in the center. Draw lines emanating from the circle like spokes from a wheel. On each line write a subordinate detail.

detail   detail

detail   **MAIN IDEA**

detail   detail

detail

- Underline the most important point in each paragraph.

- List the events that took place, in correct order.

- Make a chart comparing and contrasting main ideas.

- List the important facts in order of their importance.

- Remove all descriptive phrases.

- Circle any words you're unable to figure out from the context (**con**nected **text**).

  * Write these on individual index cards.

3x5

front   **word**   back   **MEANING**

Interpret

- List all the conclusions you drew from the reading.

- Tell what the author meant by certain statements you think are important.

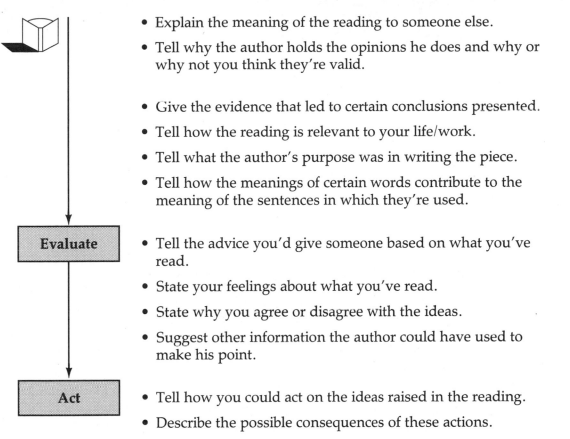

- Explain the meaning of the reading to someone else.
- Tell why the author holds the opinions he does and why or why not you think they're valid.

- Give the evidence that led to certain conclusions presented.
- Tell how the reading is relevant to your life/work.
- Tell what the author's purpose was in writing the piece.
- Tell how the meanings of certain words contribute to the meaning of the sentences in which they're used.

Evaluate

- Tell the advice you'd give someone based on what you've read.
- State your feelings about what you've read.
- State why you agree or disagree with the ideas.
- Suggest other information the author could have used to make his point.

Act

- Tell how you could act on the ideas raised in the reading.
- Describe the possible consequences of these actions.
- Tell how you could change a situation.
- Tell how you could apply the reading to your work or life.

READING COMPREHENSION MODEL: A REVIEW		
BEFORE	**DURING**	**AFTER**
• Set purpose • Preview	• Read for meaning • Use clues to predict meaning	• Recall • Interpret • Evaluate • Act

Your Turn! You've picked up a paperback on time management.

1. Before beginning to read it, state your reading purpose in the box provided. Ask yourself: Why am I reading this? What do I want to gain from this book?

Reading Purpose:

2. Read the following selection.

SETTING PRIORITIES

When opportunities exceed resources, decisions must be made. Nowhere is this more apparent than in the use of time. Since time cannot be manufactured, you must decide what to do and what not to do.

Setting priorities in the use of time is a two-step process: (1) listing things that need to be done, and
(2) prioritizing items on the list. (See facing page.)

Use the ABC method to determine your priorities by placing each item on your list into one of the following categories:

- Priority A—"Must-do": These are the critical items. Some may fall in this category because of management directives, important customer requirements, significant deadlines, or opportunities for success or advancement.

- Priority B—"Should-do": These are items of medium value. Items in this category may contribute to improved performance but are not essential or do not have critical deadlines.

- Priority C—"Nice-to-do": This is the lowest value category. While interesting or fun, they could be eliminated, postponed, or scheduled for slack periods.

Your A's, B's, and C's are flexible depending on the date your list is prepared. Priorities change over time. Today's "B" may become tomorrow's "A" as an important deadline approaches. Likewise, today's "A" may become tomorrow's "C", if it did not get accomplished in time and/or circumstances change.

Obviously, it is not worthwhile to spend considerable time on a task of modest value. On the other hand, a project of high value is worth the time invested. Only good planning will allow you to reap the benefits of time wisely invested.

Use the form on the facing page to practice setting priorities.

from *Personal Time Management* by Marion E. Haynes (reprinted with author's permission)

SETTING PRIORITIES

3. Enter your reading accomplishment in the box provided. Ask yourself: Did I find out what I wanted to?

Reading Accomplishment:

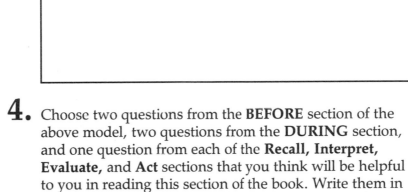

4. Choose two questions from the **BEFORE** section of the above model, two questions from the **DURING** section, and one question from each of the **Recall, Interpret, Evaluate,** and **Act** sections that you think will be helpful to you in reading this section of the book. Write them in the box below.

BEFORE: 1. _____

2. _____

DURING: 1. _____

2. _____

AFTER:

RECALL _____

INTERPRET _____

EVALUATE _____

ACT _____

☞ **ON YOUR WAY**

Cut out the bookmark below and attach it to a piece of cardboard. After frequently applying the strategies outlined in the above model, using the bookmark alone will help your active reading behaviors become automatic.

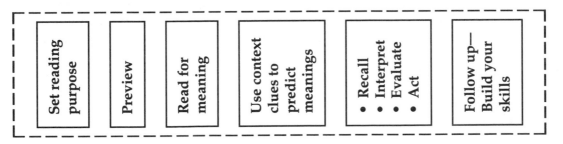

SKILL 2:
CLEARING THE AIR
Reading For Main Ideas

TOPIC   **MAIN IDEA**

A topic is a word or short phrase that answers the questions, *"What are you reading about?"*

A **main idea** is the central point of a paragraph, article, report, chapter, or book. It's the sentence or phrase that sums up what a written passage is all about. It gives more specific information than the general topic or subject of your reading.

Finding main ideas in your reading is the most important adult reading skill you can develop. You'll use it every day in your job, at home, in business transactions, and in formal test-taking situations.

Sometimes, in a short unit like a paragraph, you may find the main idea clearly stated in a topic sentence, right **upfront.**

> **EXAMPLE: Today, more older Americans want to work.** Many active older Americans are discovering that retirement isn't all it was cracked up to be—that traditional retirement can be financially risky and emotionally unsatisfying. Recent polls show that 40 percent of retired people would rather be employed outside the home than engaged involunteer or caregiving activities. In fact, large companies like 3M are now rehiring their formerly retired employees.

At other times, you'll find the main idea in a topic sentence at the **end** of a paragraph.

> **EXAMPLE:** Older American workers tend to be active and healthy and bring a wealth of practical experience to their jobs and work teams. They are reliable and stable workers, having fewer absences than their younger co-workers, good overall attendance records, and lower workplace dropout rates. They account for only a small percentage of accidents at work and illegal drug use. Their ability to handle stress lowers their risk of physical and emotional illness, helping companies that employ them maintain lower health care costs. Undoubtedly, **older workers are assets to today's corporations.**

You may also find the topic sentence buried in the **middle** of a paragraph, or *implied*—not directly stated.

In this case you have to *infer* or judge, from the details given, and their organization, what the main point is.

> **EXAMPLE:** Many older men and women would like to work late evenings or even weekends so that they could take advantage of uncrowded recreation facilities on weekdays. They'd be willing to work longer hours for a few days in order to get regular three-day weekends. Others would prefer working early mornings, freeing their afternoons for their grandchildren, shopping, gardening, or other hobbies.

MAIN IDEA = **Older people are interested in flexible work schedules.**

READING FOR MAIN IDEAS (Continued)

Reading for main ideas is *ACTIVE READING*!

Active reading requires reading with a purpose. Active reading trains your eyes and brain to work like magnets, searching out and grabbing hold of the main points or central ideas that answer the questions that prompted your reading in the first place.

Before you start reading, ask yourself:
"What's the main idea here?
What's the main point the author
wants to make?"

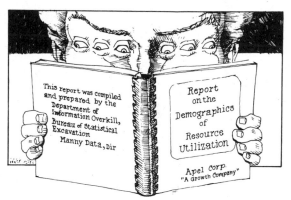

Read the entire passage, looking for the answer to your question.

After you've read the passage, state to yourself the main idea.

Your Turn! Find and underline the main idea or topic sentence in each of these passages. If you can't find a topic sentence, if the main idea is *implied,* state the main idea in your own words at the end of the passage.

1. **(a)** Not long ago, the job of a supervisor was to direct and control the work activities of his subordinates. **(b)** He scheduled vacations, doled out overtime, trained new employees, conducted performance reviews, and, in general, saw to it that the work of a department got done. **(c)** But the role of the supervisor is changing. **(d)** With an increasing number of organizations using work teams to organize and virtually run their own minifactories, the new breed of supervisor is better defined as a leader, coach, facilitator, or technical resource.

2. **(a)** A stress test has several benefits for patients recovering from heart attacks. **(b)** It can help determine proper activity levels for work and exercise. **(c)** It can identify those at risk for another attack. **(d)** And it can measure the effectiveness of medications.

3. **(a)** Some hospitals have launched aggressive advertising campaigns, plastering profiles of their own nurses on city billboards. **(b)** Teaching hospitals in large U.S. cities like Boston are joining forces to recruit new members. **(c)** Others conduct job fairs in cities several thousand miles away hoping to attract nurses to East and West Coast cities. **(d)** A South Carolina hospital pays cash awards to employees who refer nursing candidates. **(e)** Hospital personnel are going into the schools to ''talk up'' the rewards of the profession.

4. **(a)** A patient might enter a clinic and identify herself with an electronic card containing her complete computerized medical history and automatic billing information. **(b)** After responding to a series of questions posed by a computer, she would submit to a series of self-administered tests (e.g. temperature, blood pressure, urinalysis, etc.) **(c)** Finally, she might receive a preliminary diagnosis and be issued an unsigned prescription for medication. **(d)** Only when this automated process was complete, would she see a nurse or doctor. **(e)** It's possible, in the 1990's, that patients of a modern HMO might receive sophisticated diagnoses and even some forms of treatment with limited intervention of doctors, nurses, or clerical support personnnel.

(from *Workforce 2000*)

ANSWERS: 1. (c) 2. (a) 3. There's a shortage of nurses and hospitals are using a number of untraditional methods to solve the problem. 4. (e)

SKILL 3: THE BOTTOM LINE

Identifying Key Information in Memos, Letters, and Reports

MEMOS

A memo (short for memorandum) is an informal written note, used in businesses of all kinds, to communicate with workers.

Memos are used to:

- **Inform** workers of what is happening in a company.

  Example: ''You may have noticed the construction workers wandering around the cafeteria lately. On Friday afternoon, they will begin tearing down the east walls to enlarge the room.''

- **Direct** workers what to do when changes are being made.

  Example: ''Please avoid using the vending machines and tables in the area during the remodeling project.''

- **Remind** workers of company policies or procedures.

  Example: ''It's important at this time that you observe your assigned lunch hours.''

Memos can also:

- **Announce** meetings, inspections, promotions
- **Introduce** new employees, products, safety regulations

Almost always, a memo has at least one important or **key message** for you, the worker.

Each time you receive a memo, you need to read it right away, and find (identify) that bottom-line or **key message** the writer is delivering to you.

---

7 STEPS TO MEMO MASTERY

Please do the following things each time you receive a memo:

1. Read the whole memo carefully—including the *name* of the writer and the *date* it was written. Pay particular attention to the ''*Subject*,'' or word(s) following ''*Re:*.''

2. Underline any words you don't know (including technical terms and abbreviations). Look them up in your dictionary, and write them down, along with their meanings, at the bottom of the memo. If you can't find the meanings, ask a friend.

3. Find/Identify the **key message** (or messages) that pertains to you and "box it off" (draw a box around it).

To locate the key message, it helps to

Ask yourself:

- *What does this mean for me?*
- *What do I need to do?*
- *How do I need to change what I'm doing now?*

4. Then look for and identify the **details** accompanying the key message and highlight them with a marker.

Ask yourself:

- *When* do I need to do this?
- *Where* do I need to do this?
- *With whom* do I need to do this?
- *Why?*

5. Watch for, and circle **"cue words"** or phrases that may lead you to the **bottom-line message** or give you the details.

Examples:

—after	—no later than	—in order that
—as soon as	—whenever	—regarding
—during	—however	—to sum up
—from now on	—in addition	—unless
—immediately	—instead of	

6. Jot down any questions you have about the information you've read, and ask your supervisor, work unit leader, or a friend for, explanations.

7. Act on the writer's message—or file the memo if you'll need to refer to it later.

MEMOS (Continued)

In short: The best strategy is to ACT!

<u>A</u>sk and answer any questions you may have about the memo.

<u>C</u>oncentrate on the main message or messages of the writer.

<u>T</u>ake the required action.

WHY READ MEMOS?

Reading and understanding memos helps you:
- Know what's going on around you
- Comply with company rules
- Do your job correctly
- Prevent accidents
- Respond quickly and confidently to changes in directions, work processes, equipment, materials
- Keep your job

Here is a model you can use in applying the **7 STEPS TO MEMO MASTERY** (from page 14–15) to your own memo reading.

TO: Policyowner Service Clerks
FROM: Rachel Jones
DATE: February 14
SUBJECT: Customer Service "Breaks"

It has come to my attention that phones are not being answered <u>expediently</u> over the ~~lunch hours~~ and during A.M. breaks. Many phone calls have been coming in <u>simultaneously</u>, creating a build-up in the <u>tank</u> and increasing our department's monthly <u>lag</u> stats.

I'd like to <u>reiterate</u> the <u>crucial</u> importance of assuming responsibility for answering any ringing phone, even if it's not yours. Keep in mind that good ~~public relations~~ requires our company to be <u>accessible</u> by telephone at all times.

Also, remember to use FORM 539 to take messages, recording the date, time, name, and telephone number, repeating the number for verification if necessary. I'm asking for your ~~joint~~ cooperation in correcting this problem immediately.

EXAMPLE: You may need to find and write the meanings of the following words:

expediently – in a way that is advantageous

simultaneously – at the same time

tank – part of a phone system that holds incoming phone calls

lag stats – statistics showing how long it takes to service incoming phone calls

reiterate – repeat

crucial – critical, very important

accessible – able to reach easily

verification – confirmation, establishing the truth

Your Turn! 1. Please read the following memo. Then complete the **7 STEPS TO MEMO MASTERY** as shown in the model memo on page 16.

DATE: July 21

RE: CARING FOR RESIDENTS WITH AIDS/HIV INFECTIONS

FROM: Steve Foster

The recent correspondence from the Division of Health regarding AIDS and HIV Infections further clarifies our responsibility as an employer and long term health care provider. This memo, resulting from the Governor's HIV/AIDS Technical Advisory Committee, specifically requires us to inform you that we as employees will be expected to care for residents having AIDS/HIV infections. The correspondence reinforces our responsibility to abide by the law (Section 504, Rehabilitation Act) which prohibits discrimination based on the disabling effects of AIDS or HIV infections.

I'm restating our commitment to the provision of these services to our residents in a manner in which is both sensitive to your concerns and protective of you as an individual. We will continue to monitor our process of preparation, care, and treatment in a manner which will address your concerns for hygiene and overall safety.

Your Turn! 2. Use a memo you have received in the past month to complete the **7 STEPS TO MEMO MASTERY**.

☞ **ON YOUR WAY**

Put each new word you've learned in a memo on a separate 3″×5″ index card.

Flip through your "deck" once a week to review the word meanings and build your vocabulary.

LETTERS

Letters differ from memos in these ways:

- They're more personal—
The greeting, ''Dear,'' involves you, the reader, directly and immediately.

- They're often used to communicate with people outside your company (external customers).

- They have a wider range of use.

In business, letters can:

- **Request an Explanation**
Example: ''Tell me why, after all these years, I had trouble returning a sweater without a receipt!''

- **Explain**
Example: ''The two clerks in that department were temporaries and were not familiar with our return policies.''

- **Complain**
Example: ''I received a lapsed policy notice even though I paid my premium on the due date!''

- **Answer a Complaint**
Example: ''We routinely register premiums on our terminals on the fifth of the month. Our records indicate receipt of your premium on the seventh of October.''

- **Thank**
Example: ''Thank you for making a special delivery of paper to our Copy Center at noon. You saved our day.''

- **Apologize**
Example: ''We regret the inconvenience caused by our delay in shipping the chemicals you requested.''

- **Give Bad News**
Example: ''After careful consideration, we've concluded that your request for an extension cannot be honored.''

- **Confirm**
Example: ''I look forward to meeting you, on the third of July, to discuss our new Retirement Plan.''

- **Sell**
Example: ''We know you'll find our new safety glasses more comfortable, durable, and attractive than our competitors'.''

Parts of a Letter

Most letters contain 3 distinct parts:

1. **OPENING:** States the **purpose** of the letter
2. **BODY:** Develops **details**
3. **CLOSE:** States the **action to be taken**, and may set **deadlines**

Many times you'll find the **bottom-line** or **key message** in the OPENING or CLOSE of the letter.

Each time you receive a business letter, complete the same 7 STEPS you take in reading a memo (p. 14–15), with one exception. Make a copy of the letter to use for your note-taking. *Letters are sometimes used as legal documents and should not be changed in any way.*

In short: **A**sk and answer any questions you may have about the letter.

Concentrate on the main message or messages of the writer.

Take the required action.

Your Turn! **1.** Please read the following letter and apply the **7 STEPS** you learned on p. 16.

May 17

Dear Ms. Jackson:

Several conversations with billing clerks in your office have resulted in no definitive action taken to adjust the inaccurate balance reflected in my monthly charge statement. Due to this error, whether deliberate or inadvertent, I'm paying a hefty finance charge based on an overcharge of $328.83—for an item I never purchased.

How many times do I have to inform you of this discrepancy before the problem is resolved? I'll call you in two days to see if and how you have rectified this situation— before contacting your superior.

Sincerely,

Maria Lopez
Maria Lopez

Your Turn! **2.** Use a letter you have received at work in the past month to complete the **7 STEPS**.

☞ ON YOUR WAY

Put each new word you've learned in a letter on a separate 3″×5″ index card.

Flip through your "deck" once a week to review the word meanings and build your vocabulary.

REPORTS

A report is a detailed account or statement. Reports differ from memos and letters because they're more formal and less personal and usually contain more details.

Reports can be used to:

1. **Inform** employees of the financial state of the company, as well as

   —the productivity of work teams and individual workers

   Example: Productivity in the Data Entry Unit rose 2.3 percent this year.

   —product defects and service gaps

   Example: Our incoming call abandon rate continues to hover at an unacceptable 4.9 percent.

   —investments and return on investments (ROI)

   Example: We realized a healthy 18 percent return on our Canadian real estate ventures.

   —health insurance costs and other employee benefits

   Example: The increasing costs of employee medical coverage are moving us to consider an employee participation plan.

   —use of company-sponsored programs

   Example: We're pleased to report a 50 percent utilization rate of our Employee Assistance Program this fiscal year.

2. **Measure** work unit and individual worker performance.

   Example: Jennifer Levarro posted a 20 percent increase in sales in the Southeast territory this month.

Reading and understanding the reports you receive can help you:

- Be aware of what's going on in the company at large
- See ways in which you can work better and faster
- Adjust your work habits to achieve these goals
- Value your contribution to the company's overall success
- Understand changes that are taking place in other areas of the company
- Communicate better with employees in other departments and external customers

REPORT SUCCESS

Our information systems technology can produce mountains of reports. Take the following steps to stay on top of them:

1. Get acquainted with the **key reports** that are routinely circulated in your company and especially in your work area.

2. Learn the purpose of each of them.

   Ask:

   - *What does this mean for me?*

   - *What do I need to do?*

   - *How does the work of other departments affect me and my job?*

   - *How and how much do I need to improve?*

3. Ask experienced co-workers about the meanings of unfamiliar words and math figures.

4. Suggest to your supervisor that various reports be discussed at weekly or monthly staff meetings.

Your Turn!

The following report was distributed to all employees of GLOBAL CYCLE Company. As a new employee of this company, what questions might you ask after reading this report?

We are pleased to report that the Just-In-Time program we introduced in all our plants last September has produced exciting and profitable results for Global Cycle. As you know, the driving force of JIT is the need to reduce cycle time—the time a factory requires to go from the raw materials stage to the shipment of finished goods. Reducing cycle time has forced us to solve problems that previously caused interruptions in our manufacturing process. As a result, we've been able to accomplish many of our key objectives. Our overall productivity has increased 31 percent, our efficiency rate in responding to customer demands has increased 25 percent, and our costs have dropped dramatically.

SKILL 4: BEHIND THE SEEN

Recognizing Tone, Point of View, and Personal Agendas

In SKILL 3, you practiced finding the bottom-line or key message in memos, letters, and reports. In the samples you worked with, the writers delivered these key messages in a pretty straightforward manner.

But people don't always come right out and say what they mean. For fear of hurting feelings, appearing dictatorial, or simply causing conflict, they may ''hedge,'' even in a memo. They may **''mask''** their remarks in a way that makes it difficult for you to know what they're really getting at, or what they want.

Because succeeding in business requires meeting management's expectations, developing a sensitivity to what's not said directly—but is implied—is an important skill. In fact, it can be almost as critical as understanding what's there on paper, in black and white!

Your Turn! How well can you read ''between the lines?'' Here's your chance to practice. Find the underlying or **''masked message''** in each of these memos.

To: All DYNO-FREIGHT Employees
From: Ray Clevers, President
Subject: ''Hoops for Health''

As you know, three star players from the Detroit Pistons will be visiting DYNO-FREIGHT next Thursday to participate in our childhood cancer fund raiser. Every employee is invited and encouraged to attend this special company event and beat the pros at their own game—all for a most worthwhile cause.

While many companies sponsor two or three such events annually, DYNO-FREIGHT takes pride in sinking all its efforts into this one opportunity to demonstrate our community involvement and goodwill.

MASKED MESSAGE: _____

_____

_____

_____

_____

To: April Reins
From: Jan McSweet

You've done an excellent job in the past year of maintaining a well-stocked inventory of supplies for the department.

Now that we've instituted our quality improvement program, you may find that this additional ''housekeeping'' responsibility interferes with your other job duties. I don't recall seeing your control charts requested last week, though I'm sure you submitted them.

MASKED MESSAGE: _____

_____

To: Printers' Products Sales Reps
From: Lou Stake
Subject: Literature Update

Attached is an updated listing of available Printers' Products literature. Regular turnaround time on literature ordering is 10–12 working days. Rush orders will be charged to branch budgets and require sales management approval.

LITERATURE ORDERS CANNOT BE TAKEN OVER THE PHONE.

Thank you for your cooperation.

MASKED MESSAGE: _____

_____

To: Claire Wicks
From: Alberto Rivas
Subject: CENTRAIL Account

My boss recently questioned me about the CENTRAIL account, wondering why sales to this key client of ours have dropped 43 percent in the first quarter.

I know you'll brief me on this matter at the conclusion of your training activities.

MASKED MESSAGE: _____

_____

ANSWERS: 1. ''Every employee is *expected* to attend this event. I'll be on the lookout!'' 2. ''Get your priorities straightened out! You should know how important this program is to me and the company.'' 3. ''Don't inconvenience me with rush orders. If you do, you'll have to answer to your boss. And whatever you do, don't call requesting the literature.'' 4. ''Brief me on this account now—before I lose my job and you do too!''

SKILL 5: TRAILBLAZERS

Simplifying Instructions

Instructions, directions, and procedures all tell you **HOW TO DO** something—how to perform a particular set of tasks to achieve a goal.

Since you were very young, you've learned to accomplish many difficult tasks by following instructions.

Whatever kind of job you have, your duties will often require you to <u>read instructions</u> and <u>follow them</u> in order to complete a particular task correctly.

Sometimes instructions are written in an orderly, easy-to-understand format.

Example:
1. Complete, sign, and date the HCRA (Health Care Reimbursement Account) Claim Form.
2. Attach any documentation that describes the nature of the expense.
3. Mail the HCRA Claim Form and documentation to BODEWELL'S Benefits Department.

At other times they're written in paragraph form and can seem overwhelming to the inexperienced worker.

But you can learn to <u>simplify instructions</u>—make them easier to use—by separating them into manageable parts and applying the following steps. These steps will help you "blaze a trail" to the specific actions you need to take to complete the task.

1. **T**ake a <u>positive</u>, confident "I can master this" <u>attitude</u> toward the instructions. *(Remember: You've done it successfully before!)*

2. **R**ead all the instructions from beginning to end, <u>to get the whole picture</u> before jumping in to perform any one step.

3. **A**sk yourself—<u>and</u> be able to <u>answer</u>:

   • *<u>What exactly am I being asked to do here?</u> What do I need to accomplish?*

   • *<u>Why?</u> What is the desired result or end product? What will the "finished product" look like? Why is it important?*

4. **I**dentify unfamiliar words, technical terms, abbreviations, and acronyms. Look them up in your dictionary, and write them down, along with their meanings, at the bottom of the instructions sheet before proceeding.

5. **L**ocate—and keep handy—additional
   - materials (procedure manuals, blueprints, forms, directories)
   - equipment (calculator, date stamper)
   - information (computer printouts, specifications)

   you need to perform the task.

6. **S**ingle out the *action words*, or verbs, used in the instructions. Give them your special attention. These are the words that tell you most directly what to do. Think of these words as *flashing lights* signaling the actions you need to take.

> **Examples:** *Transfer* the call.
> *Load* the containers.
> *Date stamp* the envelopes.
> *Review* the screen.

If the instructions are written in paragraph form, break them up into individual steps, one to a line and introduced by a verb.

After completing these six steps, after "blazing your **TRAILS**":

- Complete each step of the instructions in their correct order—

  and

  if you'll need to use the instructions regularly,

- Create your own "job aid" to help you remember the steps you need to take to perform the task.

Janine read the following instructions for making service calls when she inherited duties as a key operator:

> ### SERVICE CALLS
>
> As the key operator for your department, it is your responsibility to see that the copy machine located in your area remains functional. If the copy machine should stop working, please consult your KEY OPERATOR REFERENCE GUIDE to identify the problem (for example, main tray misfeeds or fuser jam.) Be sure to record your meter reading before calling the Lead Technician, at Extension 1088, to identify your department, floor, and machine model number and give your meter reading. Posting an "out of order" sign on your machine, if it is inoperable, will preclude people making futile trips to the machine, and possibly, the need for additional repairs.

Simplifying Instructions (Continued)

This is the job aid Janine created for easy reference when the copy machine broke down:

When the copy machine isn't working properly:

1. <u>Identify</u> the <u>problem</u> (maintray misfeeds, fuser jam, etc.).
2. <u>Record</u> the <u>meter reading</u>.
3. <u>Call Lead Technician</u>.
   a. Give department, floor, machine model number (#1100).
   b. Give meter reading.
   c. State the problem.
4. <u>Put</u> an "<u>out of order</u>" <u>sign</u> on machine if it can't be used.

Apply the above six steps (**TRAILS**) to a set of instructions or procedures you've recently received. Then create a job aid based on these instructions for use in your department.

Here is a list of action words, VERBS, commonly used in instructions or procedures:

obtain order receive request retain secure	analyze audit check compare edit evaluate examine scan screen verify	arrange assemble collate compile file gather match merge separate	calculate consult determine estimate identify measure reference sample tally
code document draft indicate inform log note record register report state	adjust align attach balance convert credit deposit depress dilute insert orient post reimburse reinstate remove vary withdraw	cancel decline delete deliver deposit direct distribute forward install provide refer reject release retrieve return route submit suspend transfer transmit transport withdraw	complete create enter establish maintain reinforce revise terminate

ACTION:

1. Circle all words you're not familiar with.

2. Learn to pronounce each of these words correctly.

3. Learn the meanings of these words.

4. For each of the words you've circled, write a one-sentence instruction that begins with the word.

SKILL 6: EYE-OPENERS

Tables and Graphs

Tables and Graphs show—visually display—information in a condensed form. They're time-savers, because they:

- Present data in a direct, precise, efficient way

- Encourage the reader's eye to compare pieces of data—to see more readily their meanings and relationships

Imagine, for a minute, plowing through a TV guide written in a standard sentence/paragraph format. Or searching for yesterday's baseball scores in a sea of straight copy.

Tables and graphs can help us better understand complex information by presenting it graphically, but interpreting them correctly requires developing a few habits and skills.

To Read a Table Correctly

1. Look at the **title**—the subject of the table. It tells you what the table's about.

2. Look at the **column headings**. They state the kinds of facts listed in each column.

3. Identify any **words or symbols** you're not familiar with. Find out and jot down their meanings before moving on.

   (Tables and graphs don't provide the clues to word meanings that are available in sentences and paragraphs.)

4. Compare the **numbers** (or other data) entered in one column with those entered under the other column headings.

5. Draw one or more **conclusions** from the data presented.

---

1. title: **MONTHLY CUMULATIVE TOTALS**

2. column headings:

MONTH	SALES	RETURNS	NET SALES
January	$2,661.03	$551.00	$2,110.03
February	$3,550.50	$640.20	$2,910.30

3. unfamiliar word: cumulative–increasing, enlarging by successive addition

4. number comparison

5. Conclusion: February net sales were $800.27 or 38% higher than January net sales.

Ask yourself:

- *What have I learned from studying this table?*
- *What do I want to remember?*

Table 3-7
THE CHANGING OCCUPATIONAL STRUCTURE, 1984-2000

Occupation	Current Jobs (000s)	New Jobs (000s)	Rate of Growth (Percentage)
Total	105,006	25,952	25
Service Occupations	16,059	5,957	37
Managerial and Management-Related	10,893	4,280	39
Marketing and Sales	10,656	4,150	39
Administrative Support	18,483	3,620	20
Technicians	3,146	1,389	44
Health Diagnosing and Treating Occupations	2,478	1,384	53
Teachers, Librarians, and Counselors	4,437	1,381	31
Mechanics, Installers, and Repairers	4,264	966	23
Transportation and Heavy	4,604	752	16
Engineers, Architects, and Surveyors	1,447	600	41
Construction Trades	3,127	595	19
Natural, Computer, and Mathematical Scientists	647	442	68
Writers, Artists, Entertainers, and Athletes	1,092	425	39
Other Professionals and Paraprofessionals	825	355	43
Lawyers and Judges	457	326	71
Social, Recreational, and Religious Workers	759	235	31
Helpers and Laborers	4,168	205	5
Social Scientists	173	70	40
Precision Production Workers	2,790	61	2
Plant and System Workers	275	36	13
Blue Collar Supervisors	1,442	−6	0
Miners	175	−28	−16
Hand Workers, Assemblers, and Fabricators	2,604	−179	−7
Machine Setters, Operators, and Tenders	5,527	−448	−8
Agriculture, Forestry, and Fisheries	4,480	−538	−12

Source: Hudson Institute

Your Turn!   1. a. What three occupations will grow the fastest between 1984 and 2000?

b. In which occupations will jobs decline the most?

c. How many more new jobs will be available in the health care field than in precision production?

ANSWERS: a. lawyers and judges, natural, computer, and mathematical scientists, health diagnosing and treating b. agriculture, forestries, fisheries, machine setters, operators, tenders c. 1,323,000

Reading Graphs

To Read a Graph Correctly

1. Look at the **title** to determine the subject of the graph—what it's about.

2. Look for a **key** (or ledger) that explains the shading or other techniques used to differentiate the items, groups, etc., being compared.

3. Read the **labels** on the horizontal and vertical lines (line and bar graphs).

4. Compare the heights and lengths of the bars and corresponding **numbers** (bar graphs). In line graphs, associate the amounts shown on the vertical axis with the dates (or other numbers) on the horizontal axis.

5. Draw one or more **conclusions** from the data presented. State the main point(s) of the graph in your own words.

   Example: "By the year 2000, the average age of people in the U.S. will be 36, eight years older than it was in 1970, and almost 10 years older than it was in 1930."

   or

   "The average age of people in the U.S. has risen steadily since 1970. This trend will probably continue."

PIE GRAPH/ (CIRCLE GRAPH)   In a pie or circle graph, the circle represents an entire unit. The parts of the circle (pieces of the pie) represent <u>portions</u> of the unit.

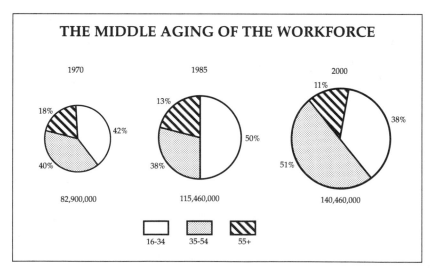

THE MIDDLE AGING OF THE WORKFORCE

1970   1985   2000

18% 42% 13% 50% 11% 38%

40% 38% 51%

82,900,000   115,460,000   140,460,000

16-34   35-54   55+

As you can see, each of these pie graphs represents the American workforce during a given year. The individual sections of the pies represent the relative portions of young, middle-aged, and older workers.

Unlike tables, **graphs** show movements, trends, and distributions.

LINE GRAPH

THE U.S. POPULATION IS GROWING OLDER
(MEDIAN AGE)

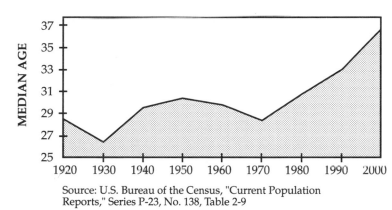

Source: U.S. Bureau of the Census, "Current Population
Reports," Series P-23, No. 138, Table 2-9

The horizontal line usually represents time.

The vertical line represents amounts or numbers of something
(people, temperature, ages, etc.) and is labeled—so you'll
recognize it easily.

BAR GRAPHS   **Bar graphs** are vertical or horizontal bars that vary in length
to represent a quantity.

**vertical bar
graph**

**MOST NEW ENTRANTS TO THE LABOR FORCE WILL
BE NON-WHITE, FEMALE OR IMMIGRANTS**

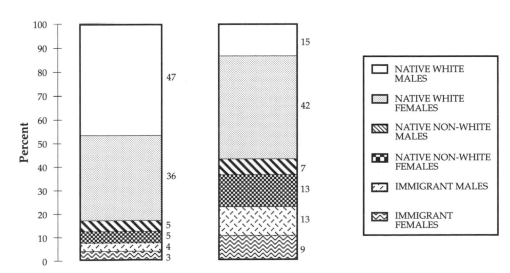

Tables and Graphs (Continued)

BAR GRAPHS (Continued)

horizontal bar graph

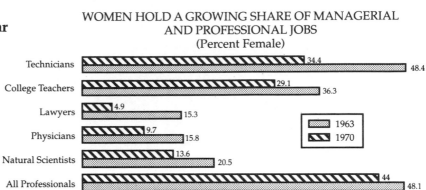

WOMEN HOLD A GROWING SHARE OF MANAGERIAL
AND PROFESSIONAL JOBS
(Percent Female)

	1963	1970
Technicians	48.4	34.4
College Teachers	36.3	29.1
Lawyers	15.3	4.9
Physicians	15.8	9.7
Natural Scientists	20.5	13.6
All Professionals	48.1	44
Accountants & Auditors	38.7	24.6
Purchasing Managers	23.6	8.5
Executive/Administrative	32.4	18.5

2. What percent of the workforce was middle aged in 1985?

What percent will be in this age group in the year 2000?

ANSWERS: 38 percent, 51 percent

☞ ON YOUR WAY

Clip tables and graphs from the newspaper and tape them to index cards for study. Apply the five steps you learned above for reading tables and graphs.

Can you obtain a copy of your organization's annual report? If so, look for tables and graphs in it.

Enter below some interesting facts you learned about your organization from examining these graphics.

SKILL 7: USING NEWS HOOKS

The Five W's and an H

Reporters write news stories in a special way called the "inverted pyramid" style. They start with the end or climax of the story, placing the important facts first. Then they build in more details in the order of their importance.

Knowing about the newspaper's "inverted pyramid" style will help you sift facts—pick out the main elements of the news story quickly.

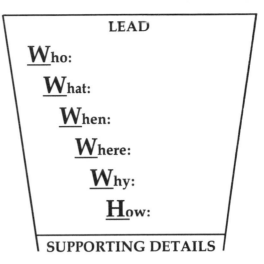

Just like hooks in your closet or on your walls can help clear a room's clutter, these "five W's and an H" can help you establish order in your reading. Once you've dealt with the most significant facts, your way is cleared to consider the supporting elements or background.

Think of the "five W's and an H" each time you begin to read a news story. Look how doing so simplifies the reading of this story that appeared in a company newsletter.

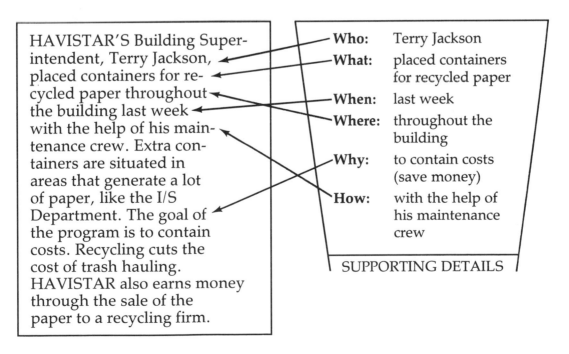

USING NEWS HOOKS (Continued)

Your Turn! **1.** Find the "five W's and H" in these news stories—using the above models.

1

An unprecedented number of WEBCO employees turned out at the Boise Blood Center March 8, where they donated a total of 93 pints of blood. Duane Haffer was giving for the first time for WEBCO, though he's donated blood before. "I know it's helping somebody. Maybe it will even help me in the future," he commented.

Who:

What:

When:

Where:

Why:

2

Connery honored

Princess Anne presented actor **Sean Connery** an award for his "outstanding contribution to world cinema."

Connery, only the third recipient of the Silver Mask Tribute Award, said he was "very moved" by the presentation Sunday in London.

Who:

What:

When:

Where:

Why:

How:

2 ANSWERS:
Who: Sean Connery
What: received award
When: Sunday
Where: London
Why: contribution to world cinema
How: from Princess Anne

1 ANSWERS:
Who: WEBCO employees
What: donated blood
When: March 8
Where: Boise Blood Center
Why: to help those in need of it

S E C T I O N

II

WORKING VOCABULARY

Use this section as a reference tool to better understand your work environment. All pages in this section have been marked "REFERENCE" for your convenience.

SKILL 8: BEYOND BYTE FRIGHT

Decoding Computer Jargon

"Bugs" and "bytes," and "fiche" and "chips." Welcome to computer country and **computerese**—the fascinating (often baffling) "language" or jargon used by computer and information systems specialists! Settle in, become comfortable with the following terms. Learning their meanings, and how to use them correctly, will help to increase your confidence—and competence—on the job.

General Computer Terms:

- **bit** = a binary digit (1 or 0) - the smallest possible unit of information a computer can work with

- **byte** = group of 8 bits

- **character** = a single letter, number, punctuation mark, space, or symbol stored or processed by a computer; examples: E, 5, ?, *

- **command** = an instruction to the computer

- **cursor** = a small light on a visual display screen (monitor) that indicates the place where data can be entered, deleted, or changed

- **data** = any information (facts, numbers, letters) the computer can use to be stored, output, or computed

- **data processing** = one or more operations performed on data to make it useful to users (workers who use computers or their output)

- **debug** = to correct the errors in a computer program

- **hardware** = the physical components or equipment that make up a computer system, like a keyboard, floppy disk drive, and visual display

- **software** = the programs or instructions that tell a computer what to do

- **key** = to enter data into a system using a keyboard

- **menu** = a list of actions from which you can choose what you want a computer program to do, like "save," "print," "center," "erase," etc.

- **mouse** = a small box with buttons attached to a computer that's used to move the cursor, data, diagrams, or other objects around on the display screen

- **password** = a special word, code, or symbol that a user must key into a terminal to enter or access data

- **PC** = personal computer

- **response time** = the time it takes a computer system to react to a particular input

- **terminal** = a screen and a keyboard (visual display unit)

BEYOND BYTE FRIGHT (Continued)

Types of Computers

- **micro computer** = a small computer usually used by only one person at a time
- **mini computer** = a computer that's usually larger than a microcomputer but with not as much power as a mainframe
- **mainframe** = a medium-to large-sized computer, usually having some peripheral devices (printer, disk), that can run several programs at the same time. May have several smaller computers connected to it.

PARTS OF A COMPUTER

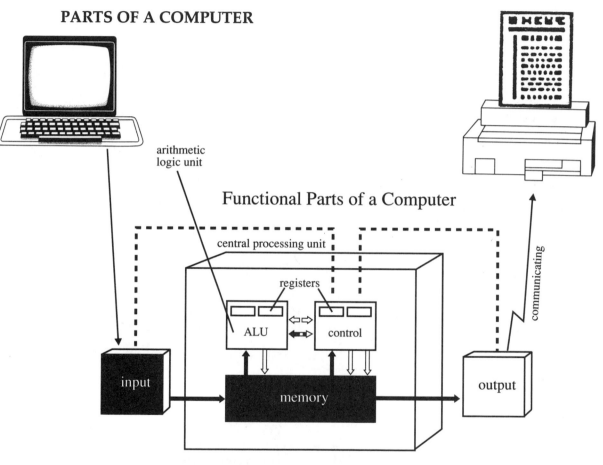

Functional Parts of a Computer

- **input** = the information a computer takes into its main storage unit from an input or storage device
- **processing** = the computer's "handling" of data to obtain a specific result
- **output** = data that's transferred from a computer's internal storage unit to some storage or output device. Also, the final result of data processed by the computer.
- **storage** = where information is stored, either in a computer or on an external device such as a floppy disk
- **communicating** = process of sending information to a point of use

Input Terms:

- **input device** = a unit used to enter data into a computer, like a keyboard
- **edit** = to check the accuracy of data or change its form by adding or deleting characters (letters, punctuation marks, etc.)
- **VDT** (<u>v</u>ideo <u>d</u>isplay <u>t</u>erminal) = device for entering information into a computer and showing it on a screen
- **CRT** (<u>c</u>athode <u>r</u>ay <u>t</u>ube) = device like a TV screen; picture tube of a video display terminal; also referred to as a monitor

Processing Terms:

- **batch** = a group of records or programs that is treated as a single unit for processing on a computer
- **Lotus 1-2-3** = an integrated software system with three functions: electronic spreadsheet, data base functions, and graphics
- **microchip** = tiny silicon (chemical) wafer containing thousands of circuits etched onto its surface
- **microprocessor** = the basic arithmetic, logic, and control elements needed for processing, usually contained on one circuit chip
- **operating system** = the group of programs which controls how a computer works. It may load programs to be run, open and close files, maintain libraries, schedule, debug, perform accounting functions, etc.
- **program** = series of instructions that tell a computer what to do
- **programming language** = formal system of notation used by a designer, writer, and tester of compugrams (programmer) to tell a computer to do a specific job

---

Common Programming Languages

PASCAL—	used to teach good methods of structured programming
COBOL—	<u>Co</u>mmon <u>B</u>usiness <u>O</u>riented <u>L</u>anguage-most commonly used computer language, best suited to business computing
BASIC—	<u>B</u>eginner's <u>A</u>ll-purpose <u>S</u>ymbolic <u>I</u>nstruction <u>C</u>ode-easy to learn and use algebraic language
FORTRAN—	<u>For</u>mula <u>Tran</u>slator-used to perform scientific, mathematical, and engineering computations
Report Generator—	changes machine-readable data into a printed report

BEYOND BYTE FRIGHT (Continued)

Output Terms:

- **microfiche** = a sheet of microfilm (about 4×6 inches) on which the images of computer output are recorded. Used for long-term storage of information like medical records, or newspapers

- **bar-code** = code used on labels read by a scanner (in the supermarket, library, etc.)

- **universal product code** = 10-digit code used in labeling retail products (5-digit manufacturer ID number and 5-digit product code number) that can be read by a computer

Storage Terms:

- **memory** = part of the computer that stores instructions and data; the amount of instructions and data a computer can store
- **boot** = to "start up" a program, move it into the computer's memory
- **disk** = a platter used to store data and programs. Information is stored magnetically in circles called tracks.
    - **—hard disk** = rigid platter that can store several million characters of information
    - **—floppy disk** = small, thin, flexible platter that can store about 250,000 characters, and is usually used only on micro- and mini-computers
- **disk drive** = device that reads information from a magnetic disk or copies it onto the disk (recording it into the computer's memory) so that it can be used by the computer
- **tape** = strip of material with a magnetically-sensitive surface used for data input, storage, or output
- **RAM—R**andom **A**ccess **M**emory = main or working memory of the computer that stores information *temporarily* while the computer's being used
- **ROM—R**ead **O**nly **M**emory = the part of memory that contains information that the computer uses *repeatedly*
- **data structures** = relationships among the elements of information in a computer file
- **data base** (D-BASE) = a common pool of related records or files used as a central file for many data processing applications

- **file** = a collection of information stored on a disk
- **field** = one piece of data in a record, like a name or amount of money
- **transaction** = an event that produces data that needs to be entered into a system (payment of a bill, for example) or the actual data that's been entered into the system

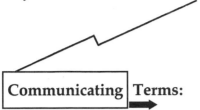

Communicating Terms:

- **baud** = rate of telecommunication transmission (usually 1200, 2400, or 9600 bits per second)
- **modem** = telephone line interface between computers
- **network** = a system of interconnected computer systems and terminals
- **LAN**—**L**ocal **A**rea **N**etwork = a network of computer systems confined to a small area (room, building, etc.)
- **WAN**—**W**ide **A**rea **N**etwork = any network connected with commercial telecommunications lines

☞ **ON YOUR WAY**

List the kinds of output generated in your work unit or department by computers.

1. What kind of data is keyed into the computer terminals?

2. What comes out?

3. How is the output used by your company/organization?

SKILL 9: IN BRIEF

Abbreviations and Acronyms

Abbreviation = shortened form of a word or phrase

    Examples: **in.** = inch

                    UPS = United Parcel Service

Acronym = word formed by placing, in order, the first letters of words in a phrase or title

    Examples: **laser** = <u>l</u>ight <u>a</u>mplification by <u>s</u>timulated <u>e</u>mission of <u>r</u>adiation

                    BASIC = <u>B</u>eginner's <u>A</u>ll-Purpose <u>S</u>ymbolic <u>I</u>nstruction <u>C</u>ode

Many abbreviations and some acronyms are so common and easily understood that we don't think twice when we meet them in our reading.

We're not familiar with others because our work or lifestyles don't require it. For example, do you know what the **MIB** is? Probably not, unless you work in the insurance industry.

Workers in the underwriting area of an insurance company aren't stumped when they see this acronym: **MIB**. They know it stands for <u>M</u>edical <u>I</u>nformation <u>B</u>ureau, a service that files and provides medical information on insurance applicants. However, they might be puzzled by **SPC**, the abbreviation for Statistical Process Control or **JIT** (Just-In-Time), two quality improvement programs used in manufacturing.

The following lists will acquaint you with some of the common abbreviations and acronyms used:

- at work
- in business transactions
- in newspapers and magazines
- in daily living.

ABBREVIATIONS AND ACRONYMS

abbr. = abbreviation
abr. = abridged
add. = addendum
admin. = administration
amt. = amount
anon. = anonymous
a/o = account of
approx. = approximate/ly
appt. = appointment
arr. = arrive
avg./av. = average
ASAP = as soon as possible
ASL = American Sign Language
assn/assoc. = association
asst. = assistant
ASTD = American Society For Training and Development
ASTD = att./attn. = attention
att./attn. = attention
AV = audio-visual

B.A. = Bachelor of Arts
BFOQ = bona fide occupational qualification
bldg. = building
bros. = brothers

CB = citizens band
CCTV = closed circuit television
CD = certificate of deposit
CEO = chief executive officer
CFO = chief financial officer
chap. = chapter
CLU = chartered life underwriter
Co./Com. = company
COD = cash on delivery
COO = chief operating officer
corp. = corporation
COS = cash on shipment
CPA = certified public accountant
CPI = consumer price index
CPR = cardiopulmonary resuscitation
CPU = central processing unit
CRT = cathode ray tube

DA = district attorney
dd. = delivered
dep. = depart
dept. = department
dir. = director
DOB = date of birth
doz. = dozen
DP = data processing

ea. = each
EAP = employee assistance program
ed. = edition
EE/AA = equal employment/affirmative action
EFT = electronic funds transfer
e.g. = Lat: exemplum gratia (for example)
elem. = elementary
EM = electronic mail
EMT = emergency medical technician
Eng. = English/England
ER = emergency room
ESL = English as a Second Language
ET = Eastern Time
exam. = examination
exec. = executive

FYI = for your information

gds. = goods
GED = Graduate Equivalency Diploma
Gr. = Greek
gtd. = guaranteed

HA = Hospital Administration
Hb = hemoglobin
hgt. = height
hgwy. = highway
HR = Human Resources

ABBREVIATIONS AND ACRONYMS (Continued)

ICU = intensive care unit
id. = Lat.: idem (the same)
i.e. = Lat.: id est (that is)
illus. = illustrated
inc. = incorporated
insp. = inspected
intl. = international
I/S = Information Systems
IV = intravenous

lab. = laboratory
Lat. = Latin
lb. = pound
ld. = load
LPN = licensed practical nurse

MBA = Master of Business
  Administration
mdse. = merchandise
mfg. = manufacturing
mktg. = marketing
mgr. = manager

N/C = no charge
nt. wt. = net weight

orig. = original
OT = occupational therapy
oz. = ounce

PA = public address
paren. = parenthesis
PB = passbook
pd. = paid
pg. = page
Ph.D. = Doctor of Philosophy
pkg. = package
pmt. = payment
pop. = population
prem. = premium

prep. = preparation
pres. = president

PST = Pacific Standard Time
PT = physical therapy
pt. = pint

qt. = quart
quot. = quotation

R & D = Research and Development
R and R = rest and relaxation
re: = regarding
rec. = receipt
rep = representative
RN = registered nurse
rpm = revolutions per minute
rte. = route
RV = recreational vehicle

SASE = self-addressed, stamped
  envelope
SAT = Scholastic Aptitude Test
shpt. = shipment
SNF = skilled nursing facility
SOP = standard operating procedure
std. = standard
supv. = supervisor

temp. = temperature
TM = trademark
typo. = typographical error

UV = ultraviolet

VCR = videocassette recorder
VDT = video display terminal
vocab. = vocabulary
vol. = volume
VP = vice president

AA	=	Alcoholics Anonymous
AAP	=	Affirmative Action Program
AARP	=	American Association of Retired People
AMA	=	American Medical Association
BBB	=	Better Business Bureau
BIA	=	Bureau of Indian Affairs
COBRA	=	Consolidated Omnibus Budget Reconciliation Act
DPH	=	Department of Public Health
DPT	=	Department of Public Transportation
DPW	=	Department of Public Works
EEOC	=	Equal Employment Opportunity Commission
ERA	=	Equal Rights Amendment
ERISA	=	Employment Retirement Income Security Act
FAA	=	Federal Aviation Administration
FBI	=	Federal Bureau of Investigation
FCC	=	Federal Communications Commission
FDA	=	Food and Drug Administration
FDIC	=	Federal Deposit Insurance Corporation
FHA	=	Federal Housing Administration
FRB	=	Federal Reserve Board
FTC	=	Federal Trade Commission
HEW	=	Department of Health, Education, and Welfare
HUD	=	Housing and Urban Development
IRS	=	Internal Revenue Service
NAIC	=	National Association of Insurance Corporations
NASA	=	National Aeronautics and Space Administration
NLRD	=	National Labor Relations Board
OAS	=	Organization of American States
OBRA	=	Omnibus Budget Reconciliation Act
OEO	=	Office of Economic Opportunity
OFCCP	=	Office of Federal Contract Compliance Programs
OPEC	=	Organization of Petroleum Exporting Countries
OSHA	=	Occupational Safety and Health Act
PHA	=	Public Housing Authority
SBA	=	Small Business Administration
SSA	=	Social Security Administration
TEFRA	=	Tax Equity and Fiscal Responsibility Act
UN	=	United Nations
USDA	=	United States Department of Agriculture
VA	=	Veterans' Administration
VNA	=	Visiting Nurses Association

IN BRIEF (Continued)

Please review/study the above lists of abbreviations and acronyms. Then complete this exercise, referring to the list when necessary.

The following messages appeared in EM. In the spaces below each VDT, write the full form of each abbreviation.

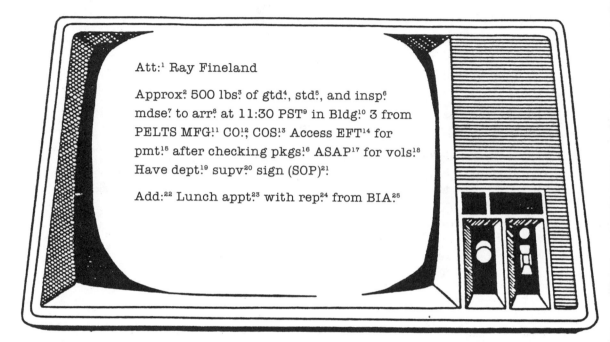

Att:[1] Ray Fineland

Approx[2] 500 lbs[3] of gtd[4], std[5], and insp[6] mdse[7] to arr[8] at 11:30 PST[9] in Bldg[10] 3 from PELTS MFG[11] CO[12], COS[13] Access EFT[14] for pmt[15] after checking pkgs[16] ASAP[17] for vols[18] Have dept[19] supv[20] sign (SOP)[21]

Add:[22] Lunch appt[23] with rep[24] from BIA[25]

1. _____   10. _____   19. _____

2. _____   11. _____   20. _____

3. _____   12. _____   21. _____

4. _____   13. _____   22. _____

5. _____   14. _____   23. _____

6. _____   15. _____   24. _____

7. _____   16. _____   25. _____

8. _____   17. _____

9. _____   18. _____

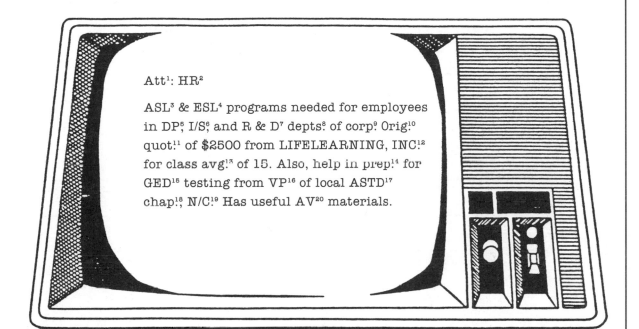

Att[1]: HR[2]

ASL[3] & ESL[4] programs needed for employees in DP[5], I/S[6], and R & D[7] depts[8] of corp[9]. Orig[10] quot[11] of $2500 from LIFELEARNING, INC[12] for class avg[13] of 15. Also, help in prep[14] for GED[15] testing from VP[16] of local ASTD[17] chap[18], N/C[19] Has useful AV[20] materials.

1. _____   8. _____   15. _____

2. _____   9. _____   16. _____

3. _____   10. _____   17. _____

4. _____   11. _____   18. _____

5. _____   12. _____   19. _____

6. _____   13. _____   20. _____

7. _____   14. _____

Check the lists for answers.

IN BRIEF (Continued)

☞ ON YOUR WAY

Please enter in the spaces below the abbreviations and acronyms your work requires you to use regularly. Then memorize them to save daily work time.

ABBREVIATION		**MEANING** (Full Form)
_____	=	_____
_____	=	_____
_____	=	_____
_____	=	_____
_____	=	_____
_____	=	_____
_____	=	_____
_____	=	_____
_____	=	_____
_____	=	_____
_____	=	_____
_____	=	_____
_____	=	_____
_____	=	_____
_____	=	_____
_____	=	_____
_____	=	_____
_____	=	_____
_____	=	_____

SKILL 10: WORDS AT WORK

Work Word Banks

As an employee of an organization, you'll see and hear the words and technical terms below often—in your employee handbook, at department meetings, in memos, newsletters, and other company communications.

Here are some suggestions for using the following word banks:

- Obtain an organization chart to see how you fit into the ''big picture''—and how your job and department relate to others in the company.
- Learn to recognize and interpret the meanings of as many of the words as you can.
- Continue to refer to this section when you need to check on the meaning of a term that appears important to your work and employment status.

BANK I

A SIMPLE ORGANIZATION CHART

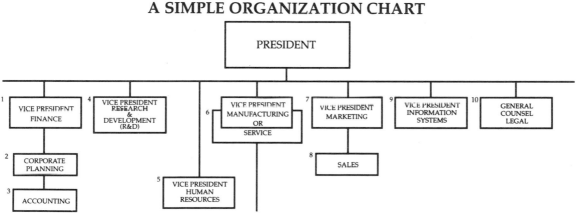

1—Oversees the flow of money in and out of an organization
2—Plans how an organization will conduct its business to achieve its objectives and fulfill its mission
3—Prepares financial statements showing a company's assets, liabilities, capital, profits and losses, etc.
4—Determines consumer needs and wants and develops new products in response
5—Writes job descriptions, recruits, interviews, hires, and trains new employees; designs and manages benefits and compensation systems, and maintains employee records
6—Produces goods or services
7—Designs, promotes, prices, and distributes goods and services
8—Sells goods or services to consumers
9—Using computers, collects, organizes, analyzes, and directs the flow of data to support the objectives of all the other units
10—Designs or examines contracts and other legal documents like patents; interprets the law as it pertains to the organization's business

WORDS AT WORK (Continued)

BANK II

HUMAN RESOURCES WORD BANK

- **employee** = a person who works for a company in exchange for wages or salary
- **recruit** = to look for and obtain new employees
- **EEO** (**E**qual **E**mployment **O**pportunity) = efforts an organization makes not to discriminate against individuals on the basis of their race, color, religion, national origin, or sex, in compliance with Title VII of the Civil Rights Act of 1964 (the federal law banning discrimination)
- **Affirmative Action** = program designed to assure equal opportunity for all persons, especially minorities
- **compensation** = money received in return for work
- **exempt** (employee) = an employee who receives a fixed salary (and doesn't receive extra pay for overtime hours)
- **non-exempt** (employee) = a worker who receives an hourly wage (and pay for overtime hours)
- **overtime** = work time that exceeds (is more than) a standard day or week
- **payroll (time) card** = a record of hours worked daily
- **FICA** (**F**ederal **I**nsurance **C**ontributions **A**ct) = the act that regulates how much of your paycheck will be paid to the federal government for taxes
- **benefits package** = the group of payments or services an organization offers its employees
- **401K Plan** = a savings/retirement plan featuring mutual contributions of the employee and employer
- **vesting** = the act by which an organization gives to an employee the right to share in the benefits of a plan, like a pension fund
- **EAP** (**E**mployee **A**ssistance **P**rogram) = a set of services an employer may offer its employees designed to help them solve personal problems that may interfere with their work performance
- **tuition reimbursement program** = program whereby an employer refunds money employees spend on education courses
- **flextime** = a system that allows employees to choose their own times for starting and finishing work within a broad range of available hours
- **sabbatical leave** = a break or change from the normal routine of employment (may be a few weeks or a few years)
- **job sharing** = two persons occupying one job (position) slot, each receiving half of the salary paid for that position
- **probationary period** = a trial period (usually about three months) to determine if an individual is fit for a job
- **subordinate** = a person who reports to someone else in charge of getting the work done

- **line** = managers and employees directly involved in the production of the final good or service the organization produces. Examples: distribution manager, inventory clerk, loan officer

- **staff** = managers and employees who advise and assist line managers and employees and are not directly involved in the production of final goods or services. Examples: training director, financial analyst, benefits clerk, PR officer

- **absence** = period during which an employee is not at work

- **tardiness** = being late for work

- **punctual** = being on time for work

- **dress code** = written or unwritten rules on what to wear at work

- **new employee orientation** = discussion sessions or presentations an organization conducts to acquaint new employees with the organization

- **policy** = an oral or written statement that guides management decisions and employee actions

    Examples: vacation policy, sick leave policy

- **procedure** = a written (usually) series of steps that spells out *how* a particular task should be performed, or how an organization's policy should be carried out (See SKILL 5)

    Examples: procedure for scheduling vacations
                    procedure for ordering supplies

- **OJT** = on-the-job training

- **corporate culture** = the prevailing customs, beliefs, values, social forms, and accepted ways of doing things in an organization—that are somewhat unique to that organization

    Example: the habit of workers "pitching in" to complete work for which they're not directly responsible

- **grapevine** = informal system of communication in an organization (i.e., gossip)

- **mentor** = a counselor, coach, or guide; a person in an organization (usually successful and in a higher position) that takes special interest in an employee's career

- **job (or position) description** = list of objectives, responsibilities, and duties for a specific position in an organization

- **job classification** = the grouping of positions into one bracket or class (called salary grade) in order to assign wages or salary

- **cross training** = training workers to handle one or more different jobs beyond those performed in their primary positions

WORDS AT WORK (Continued)

BANK III

JOB PERFORMANCE WORD BANK

- **mission statement** = written purpose of an organization's existence

    Example: *"The continuation of DOME CO. as an independently-owned, financially-strong, and growth-oriented company, dedicated to complete customer satisfaction"*

- **objective** = goal, aim, purpose, or desired result to be achieved

- **strategic planning** = an organization's long-term plan to achieve its overall objectives

- **performance standard** = a measure set up by an organization to judge an employee's work performance

    Examples: quantity = amount of work produced
    quality = accuracy of work produced

- **competency** = satisfactory performance of a work task

- **goal setting** = process of identifying the desired results a department or employee will achieve to ensure that an organization accomplishes its objectives and fulfills its mission

- **prioritize** = to arrange goals or tasks in an order from most to least urgent or important

- **performance appraisal** = the periodic (usually held every six or 12 months) review/evaluation of an employee's work performance conducted by a supervisor or manager, in collaboration with an employee, for the purpose of improving performance and determining raises and advancement opportunities for the employee

- **promotion** = the movement of an employee to a new, higher-paying position with more responsibilities

- **transfer** = the movement of an employee from one position to another, without increased duties and responsibilities

- **progressive discipline** = the process by which an organization alerts an employee to the possible consequences of inadequate work performance or behavior by giving a: 1) verbal warning; 2) first written warning; 3) second written warning

- **termination** = ending of employment with an organization

- **severance pay** = money given to an employee at the time of termination

BANK IV

ORGANIZATIONAL CHANGE WORD BANK

- **lay-off** = temporary (usually) ending of employment
- **attrition** = the process by which employees leave an organization naturally: quitting, retiring, etc.
- **downsizing** = the process by which an organization reduces the number of its employees
- **turnover** = the frequency with which employees are hired by an organization and then leave it
- **merger** = the combining of two or more organizations
- **acquisition** = the process of one company gaining or acquiring another
- **subsidiary** = a company that is controlled entirely by another company
- **holding company** = a company whose primary business is maintaining a controlling interest in the securities of other companies

BANK V

WORK GROUPS AND METHODS WORD BANK

- **participative management** = system by which employees have a voice in decisions that bear directly on their work
- **semiautonomous team** (or self-directed work team) = a largely self-governing group of workers
- **Quality Circles** (or Quality Control Circles, or employee involvement groups) = small groups of employees who volunteer to meet regularly to solve work-related problems and devise better ways of doing things.
- **ad hoc committee** = a temporary group of employees formed to complete a particular objective, after which it disbands (dissolves, breaks up)
- **task force** = an ad hoc committee whose members are drawn from various departments interested in the outcome of the task force's work
- **innovation** = introduction of something new
- **ergonomics** = study of the relationship between people and machines with the goal of designing furniture and machines to meet the safety and comfort needs of the worker. In short, the science that fits the workplace to the person using it

WORDS AT WORK (Continued)

☞ ON YOUR WAY

You'll meet many other words at work that may be strange to you. Set up your personal "word bank" below, adding such words and their meanings.

_____ _____ _____

_____ _____ _____

_____ _____ _____

_____ _____ _____

_____ _____ _____

_____ _____ _____

_____ _____ _____

"This is not the kind of perk I had in mind."
from _What's So Funny About Business?_ by Sid Harris

QUESTION: DO YOU KNOW WHAT A "PERK" IS?

SKILL 11: IT'S GOOD TO KNOW YOU

Medical and Insurance Terms

Knowing the meanings of these common medical terms will help you:

- Deal more effectively and confidently with medical personnel
- Interpret medical bills and reports
- Understand better your insurance coverage and daily reading about health-related issues
- Perform medical or insurance-related jobs more competently

COMMON MEDICAL TERMS

☐ **acetaminophen** = a non-aspirin drug used to relieve pain

☐ **acute** = used to describe an illness in which symptoms develop quickly and may disappear quickly

☐ **chronic** = used to describe a symptom or disorder that lasts a long time (weeks, months, even years)

☐ **adhesion** = fibrous scars formed when tissues heal and cause nearby organs to stick together

☐ **anesthetic** = agent that reduces or gets rid of sensation in either the whole body (general anesthetic) or a part of it (local anesthetic)

☐ **antibiotic** = drug used to fight bacterial infection

☐ **antihistamine** = drug used to fight some kinds of allergies

☐ **antiseptic** = chemical substance that destroys bacteria

☐ **benign** = a non-cancerous tumor

☐ **malignant** = a cancerous tumor

☐ **carcinogen** = any substance that can cause cancer

☐ **catheter** = a flexible tube used to remove fluids or insert them into the body

☐ **coagulant** = any substance that clots blood

☐ **communicable** = can be transmitted from one person to another

☐ **congenital** = condition or disease present at birth

☐ **cyst** = abnormal sac filled with liquid or half-solid matter

☐ **diagnosis** = process of determining what disease is present

☐ **dilation** = widening of a body opening or passageway

☐ **diuretic** = substance that reduces body fluids, increasing urine production

IT'S GOOD TO KNOW YOU (Continued)

COMMON MEDICAL TERMS (Continued)

☐ **edema** = the swelling of body tissue caused by excess water content

☐ **hemorrhage** = internal or external bleeding

☐ **immunization** = the process of the body becoming—or making it—able to fight certain diseases

☐ **metabolism** = the sum of all chemical and physical changes that take place in the body, allowing it to continue to function and grow

☐ **neonatal** = newborn

☐ **nuclear medicine** = branch of medicine that uses radioactive atomic nuclei as tracers to study and diagnose diseases

☐ **polyp** = a benign growth sticking out of a mucous membrane

☐ **prognosis** = forecast of the probable outcome of an illness

☐ **prosthesis** = artificial device used to replace a lost, natural part of the body (leg, hip joint, etc.)

☐ **remission** = disappearance of the symptoms of a chronic disease, especially cancer

☐ **toxic** = poisonous; potentially deadly

☐ **tumor** = abnormal growth of tissue that may be benign or malignant

TESTS/EXPLORATORY PROCEDURES

☐ **amniocentesis** = withdrawal of a sample of the fluid surrounding the developing fetus in the uterus to diagnose or monitor certain disorders

☐ **angiogram** = X-ray of blood vessels obtained by injecting a dye into them through a catheter

☐ **biopsy** = removal of a small piece of tissue from an organ for examination under a microscope; usually done to determine if a growth is benign or malignant

☐ **catheterization** = insertion of a flexible tube into a part of the body to obtain information on an organ's activities

☐ **CAT scan** (**C**omputerized **A**xial **T**omagraphy) = hundreds of X-rays taken by a revolving camera to obtain detailed views of body structures

☐ **ECG** or **EKG (electrocardiogram)** = a graphic recording of the electrical activity of the heart

☐ **EEG (electroencephalogram)** = a graphic recording of the electrical impulses of the brain

☐ **laparoscopy** = examination of the inside of the abdomen or female reproductive organs with a laparoscope inserted through a small incision made near the navel

☐ **laparotomy** = surgical incision into the abdominal cavity to examine the organs there in order to make a diagnosis

☐ **mammogram** = X-ray of the breast used to detect breast cancer

☐ **myelogram** = X-ray of the fluid-filled space around the spinal cord to detect tumors, displaced discs, and other disorders

☐ **ultrasound** = pictorial recording of absorbed and reflected high-frequency sound waves to reveal the interiors of organs and detect abnormalities

MEDICAL PREFIXES, SUFFIXES AND ROOT WORDS

The world of medicine has a language of its own, many of its words being derived from the Greek. Learning the meanings of these additional Greek prefixes, suffixes, and root words (see SKILL 21) will help you know how to operate when you meet even large medical terms.

- **arthro-** = joint
- **cardio-** = heart
- **cysto-** = bladder
- **derma-** = skin
- **dys-** = disordered, difficult, painful
- **ecto-** = external, outside, outer
- **-ectomy** = surgical removal
- **endo-** = internal, inside, inner
- **entero-** = intestine
- **epi-** = above, on
- **gastro-** = stomach
- **hema-** = blood
- **hernia** = rupture
- **-itis** = inflammation
- **myo-** = muscle
- **nephro-** = kidney
- **neuro-** = nerve
- **-oma** = tumor
- **-osis** = abnormal process or condition
- **osteo-** = bone
- **-pathy** = abnormality, disease
- **pneumo-** = lung; pertaining to air, gas, breathing
- **-scopy** = viewing, observing, examining
- **steno-** = narrow
- **thorax, thoraco-** = chest
- **-tomy** = surgical cutting, opening, incision
- **-uria** = urine

 **1.** Combine the appropriate prefixes, suffixes, and root words above to form the medical terms having these meanings. Use the underlined words as cues.

MEANING	MEDICAL TERM
Example: a <u>disease</u> of the peripheral <u>nerves</u>	Neuropathy

1. a <u>condition</u> in which the blood <u>clots</u> _____

2. <u>inflammation</u> of the <u>bladder</u> _____

3. <u>examination</u> of the interior of a <u>joint</u> _____

4. <u>painful</u> <u>urination</u> _____

5. <u>abnormal narrowing</u> of a passage _____

6. <u>surgical removal</u> of a <u>lung</u> _____

7. <u>on</u> top of the <u>skin</u> _____

8. <u>inflammation</u> of the <u>inner</u> lining of the <u>heart</u> muscle and valves _____

9. <u>tumor</u> or swelling containing <u>blood</u> _____

10. <u>surgical incision</u> into the <u>kidney</u> to remove a kidney stone _____

11. <u>inflammation</u> of a <u>joint</u> causing changes in the underlying <u>bone</u> _____

12. <u>abnormality</u> of the <u>muscle</u> of the <u>heart</u> _____

13. <u>surgical opening</u> between the <u>stomach</u> and the <u>intestines</u> _____

ANSWERS: 1. thrombosis 2. cystitis 3. arthroscopy 4. dysuria 5. stenosis 6. pneumonectomy 7. epidermis 8. endocarditis 9. hematoma 10. nephrotomy 11. osteoarthritis 12. cardiomyopathy 13. gastroenterostomy

Health Insurance Terms

insurer = one who covers a loss promised in a particular insurance contract

insured = one who receives payment or services for a loss covered in a particular insurance contract

benefits = dollars or services an insurance policy pays when the insured suffers a covered loss

health insurance = protection that pays benefits for sickness or injury

group insurance = provides protection for a group of people (employees, for example) through a master policy issued to an employer

disability income insurance = health insurance that makes monthly payments to replace income lost when an insured can't work because of illness or injury

☐ **beneficiary** = the person the policy names to receive the benefits of that policy

☐ **cafeteria** or **flexible benefits** plans = benefit plans in which employees can "pick and choose" additional benefits (not covered in their group insurance policy or other company fringe benefits) according to their individual needs. An employer may set up individual employee accounts to which the employer and employee contribute.

☐ **calendar year** = January 1–December 31

☐ **cancellable policy** = type of health insurance policy that allows the insurer or insured to void a policy (destroy the force of it) before it is supposed to end

☐ **claim** = the request the insured person sends to a health insurance company (insurer) for payment of an amount due under the terms of the policy

☐ **coinsurance** = sharing of the payment for covered medical expenses by the insurer and insured. A common method: insurer pays 80%, insured 20%

☐ **conditional receipt** = receipt the insurance agent gives the applicant when s/he accepts the application and full payment of the first premium from the applicant. States how the applicant will be covered until the policy is issued.

☐ **conversion privilege** = allows an insured individual to change (convert) to a different plan of insurance—without proving physical insurability—when her/his coverage by a group plan ends

☐ **coordination of benefits (COB)** = Where services are covered under more than one health insurance policy, this provision limits the benefits that can be paid on each claim to 100 percent of the expenses covered. Also specifies which company should pay the benefits first.

REFERENCE

Improve Your Reading: Improve Your Job

Health Insurance Terms (Continued)

- □ **deductible** = the amount of covered medical expenses an insured must pay "out of his/her own pocket" before her insurance policy "kicks in"—starts paying benefits

- □ **dependents** = persons who rely on an insured for financial support

- □ **diagnosis related groups (DRG)** = categories of illness that determine the amount of money hospitals receive for treating Medicare patients

- □ **dismemberment** = loss of body parts or organs through injury

- □ **effective date** = specific day when insurance coverage begins

- □ **eligibility date** = specific day on which an employee can apply for a group health insurance plan

- □ **evidence of insurability** = proof of a person's physical condition—or other facts—that determine acceptance for insurance

- □ **exclusions** = conditions, illnesses, diseases not covered by an insurance policy

- □ **explanation of benefits (EOB)** = form that tells insured persons what action the insurance company is taking on their claims; for example, why a claim is being denied or how a company will pay it

- □ **grace period** = number of days (usually 30-31), after the date the premium was due, when the insured can pay the premium without losing coverage

- □ **guaranteed renewable** = type of policy that an insurer can't cancel or change before the insured reaches a specified age

- □ **health maintenance organization (HMO)** = provides health care services to its members (subscribers) for a fixed, specified payment made at set times

- □ **incontestable clause** = states that an insurer can't challenge the validity of the insurance contract after it's been in force for two (sometimes three) years

- □ **lapsed policy** = policy that comes to an end because the insured hasn't paid the premiums

- □ **loading** = amount of money an insurer includes in a premium to allow for the insurer's expenses, taxes, profit, etc.

- □ **loss ratio** = total number of benefits an insurance company pays to its insureds divided by the total number of premiums it receives

- □ **optionally renewable** = health insurance contract in which the insurer can stop coverage at an anniversary or premium due date, but not between such dates—and not without giving the insured sufficient notice

- □ **pre-existing condition** = a physical condition (or illness, disease) that "showed up" for the first time before the insured's coverage began

- □ **premium** = amount of money an insured person pays for the benefits/protection the insurance policy provides

- ☐ **preferred provider organization (PPO)** = a group of doctors and/or hospitals that provides services to employers (or health insurers) at reduced costs, in return for prompt payment and a certain volume of patients

- ☐ **provider** = hospital, clinic, doctor, ambulance company, medical equipment company or other party that gives a medical service

- ☐ **reasonable and customary charge** (may include **usual**) = the charge for a health care service that an insurer considers to be ''in line'' with the going rate or charge for similar services in a certain geographical area

- ☐ **rider** = an addition to a policy that may increase or decrease benefits or in some other way change the coverage the policy provides

- ☐ **underwriting** = process of evaluating, classifying, and selecting risks that an insurer can cover

- ☐ **waiting period** = span of time between the date of application for coverage and the date the insurance becomes effective

- ☐ **waiver of premium** = provision in many disability income policies saying the insured no longer has to pay the premium after a specified period of disability (often total and permanent) has passed

Your Turn! Choose the terms (words or phrases) from the above list that best match the following terms (provisions of the agreement) that your insurance policy may contain. Enter them in the boxes provided.

| Your policy | **1** You pay the first $50 of your medical bills each year and I'll pay 80 percent of them after that. | Your policy | **2** I'll pay the claim just as you submitted it. The fee your doctor charged for the appendectomy is normal. |

is referring to a

[   ]

is referring to a

[   ]

Your Turn! (Continued)

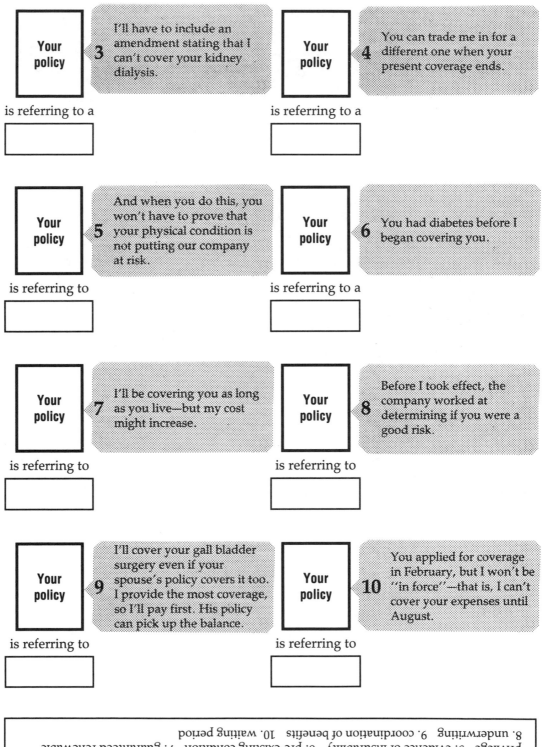

Your policy 3 — I'll have to include an amendment stating that I can't cover your kidney dialysis.

is referring to a

_____

Your policy 4 — You can trade me in for a different one when your present coverage ends.

is referring to a

_____

Your policy 5 — And when you do this, you won't have to prove that your physical condition is not putting our company at risk.

is referring to

_____

Your policy 6 — You had diabetes before I began covering you.

is referring to a

_____

Your policy 7 — I'll be covering you as long as you live—but my cost might increase.

is referring to

_____

Your policy 8 — Before I took effect, the company worked at determining if you were a good risk.

is referring to

_____

Your policy 9 — I'll cover your gall bladder surgery even if your spouse's policy covers it too. I provide the most coverage, so I'll pay first. His policy can pick up the balance.

is referring to

_____

Your policy 10 — You applied for coverage in February, but I won't be "in force"—that is, I can't cover your expenses until August.

is referring to

_____

ANSWERS: 1. deductible 2. reasonable and customary charge 3. rider 4. conversion privilege 5. evidence of insurability 6. pre-existing condition 7. guaranteed renewable 8. underwriting 9. coordination of benefits 10. waiting period

SKILL 12: IN A MANNER OF SPEAKING

DIE
IS
CAST

Figurative Language and Idioms

"The ball's in your court now!"   *"We've got to nail this down."*

"You need more ammunition."

"We're swimming upstream!"   *"Don't make waves."*

"Don't ruffle his feathers."

"It's another dog and pony show."   *"She's wet behind the ears."*

"Don't leave me in the dark."

"He's like a fish out of water."   *"What's her patient load?"*

"Bite the bullet!"

"Don't pass the buck!"   *"It's her swan song."*

"Let's hammer it out."

Where are we? On a basketball court? In the wilderness? In a tool shop or a
barnyard? At the circus, on the beach, in the army?

Well, if you're on the ball, if you don't live in an ivory tower, with your head in
the clouds, the above expressions didn't throw you for a loop. You immediately
recognized them as **FIGURES OF SPEECH**. The English language is peppered
with them!

You know figurative language. You hear it often, you use it often. Every time you
describe something by suggesting how it's like something else, you're using
figurative or metaphoric language, figures of speech.

Figures of speech like **similes** (use the words **like** or **as**) and **metaphors** (omit
these words—they're implied) suggest likenesses between two different kinds of
things by comparing them to each other.

Examples: Ever since he transferred from the machine shop to the computer
room, Joe's *like a fish out of water*.

Sophia's *razor-sharp mind* cut through the financial jargon in no time.

Sam's a *grumpy old goat*.

The computer system is a *dinosaur*.

Excellent customer service is the *key* to our success.

IN A MANNER OF SPEAKING (Continued)
Figurative Language and Idioms (Continued)

As you can see, **similes and metaphors serve important purposes in a language**. They:

- **Make it more powerful, lively, and interesting.**
- **Establish a common ground of understanding** by creating mental pictures in the mind of the reader or listener.
- **Make a point**—communicate a message—**faster and more effectively** than would be possible without them.
- Often add **humor or force** to a message.

BUT

Metaphors can also cause communication problems if you aren't familiar with the meanings of the words used in the comparisons.

> **Example:** "It's a *catch-22* situation."
> What is a "catch-22?"

When you meet a metaphor like this, before reaching for your dictionary, try to figure out the meaning of the word or phrase from the context of what you're reading or hearing.

Does this help?

> "When I have free time and offer to help him stock the shelves, he reminds me that it's his job and that he's perfectly capable of doing it himself. But when he sees me standing around with nothing to do, he complains to the manager that I'm lazy and not a team player. It's a *catch-22* situation."

In your own words, what is the meaning of "catch-22?"

> Here is one meaning: *an illogical, unreasonable, can't-win situation*

IDIOMS

Idioms are:

- **Metaphorical** phrases or sayings that can't be translated/understood literally. You can't discover their meanings by looking up the individual words in your dictionary.
- **Fixed** expressions, most often. Their grammatical forms haven't—(over time) and don't tend to—change much.
- More commonly used in **informal rather than formal** English reading and speaking, in
  —meetings
  —memos
  —letters

  —newspapers
  —magazine and trade journal articles.

Learning the meanings of idioms can be critical to understanding what goes on in the workplace and your job.

> **Example:** Your boss tells you to *"turn over a new leaf."*

While you may be able to figure out what she means from the context of the conversation, you may not.

You'll find the meaning of this idiom and 99 others, on the following list.

ABOUT 100 IDIOMS AND THEIR MEANINGS

A

- *acid test* = a test that proves beyond a doubt that someone or something isn't valuable
- *Achilles heel* = weak point
- *ax to grind* = having another, usually selfish, motive

B

- *back to square one* = back to the beginning
- *back to the drawing board* = begin again
- *The ball's in your court* = It's your turn to act.
- *beat around the bush* = avoid talking about the most important issue
- *beg the question* = avoid dealing with the point being discussed
- *behind the eight ball* = in trouble
- *between a rock and a hard place* = in a very difficult position
- *bite the bullet* = put up with something unpleasant
- *black and white* = official
- *blow the whistle* = to report a wrongdoing to someone who can stop it
- *break the ice* = get something started, overcome formality among strangers
- *bull in a china shop* = in a rough or thoughtless manner
- *burn the candle at both ends* = work hard all day and half the night too

C

- *called on the carpet* = reprimanded, scolded
- *control the purse strings* = be in charge of the money
- *corporate ladder* = series of ascending steps to important jobs/titles in an organization

D

- *devil's advocate* = person who argues against an idea even though s/he's in favor of it
- *die is cast* = an unchangeable decision is made
- *dog and pony show* = a presentation designed to impress an audience. It usually lacks substance or real value.
- *drop in the bucket* = a very small amount
- *drop the ball* = make a mistake, fail

ABOUT 100 IDIOMS AND THEIR MEANINGS (Continued)

E

- *eat humble pie* = admit you're wrong and apologize
- *eat crow* = admit you're wrong, usually in order to appear more humble

F

- *fast track* = accelerated movement to an important position in an organization
- *feather in one's cap/hat* = something to be proud of
- *fly in the ointment* = something small or unpleasant that spoils enjoyment; a drawback

G

- *glass ceiling* = invisible limit of movement to important positions in an organization (said of women and minorities)
- *Get off your high horse* = Act ordinary. Don't act superior to other people.
- *get your feet wet* = begin something new
- *give the cold shoulder* = ignore someone
- *go against the grain* = go against the natural inclination, direction, or flow of things; to irritate someone

H

- *hammer it out* = work hard at writing something
- *handwriting on the wall* = a present event that gives a clue about the outcome of a future one
- *have cold feet* = hesitate because of fear, nervousness, or uncertainty
- *high man on the totem pole* = person at the top of a hierarchy   also: **head honcho, top banana, top dog, top brass, big wig, big cheese, big wheel, captain of the ship**

I

- *in the black* = out of debt
- *in the red* = in debt

J

- *jump on the bandwagon* = go along with the crowd; do or support the popular or trendy thing
- *jump through hoops* = go out of your way to please or obey someone, usually a superior

K

- *Keep it under your hat* = keep it secret; also: **Don't let the cat out of the bag. Don't spill the beans.**
- *Keep your nose to the grindstone* = Keep busy; work hard.
- *know the ropes* = know how to do something

L

- *left holding the bag* = left to take all the blame
- *Let sleeping dogs lie* = Don't look for trouble.
- *let the grass grow under your feet* = delay, waste time
- *lie down on the job* = do a job poorly or not at all
- *life in the fast lane* = style of living that requires working, eating, shopping, and doing most everything in a hurry
- *lock, stock and barrel* = everything, completely

- *mommy track* = career path in an organization that allows a woman to work without neglecting childbearing/rearing responsibilities

N

- *nip in the bud* = stop something at an early stage

O

- *off base* = wrong, unrealistic
- *off the hook* = out of trouble
- *open a can of worms* = create unnecessary problems
- *out in left field* = out of the ordinary
- *out of the frying pan into the fire* = from a bad situation to a worse one
- *out of the woods* = out of trouble, past the critical part
- *out on a limb* = in a dangerous, risky position
- *over a barrel* = having no free choice

P

- *paper tiger* = something that outwardly appears powerful but, in fact, is ineffective
- *pass the buck* = give someone else a responsibility that's yours
- *pay your dues* = earn the right to something through hard work or hardship
- *pig in a poke* = something you buy without seeing or examining it closely; a disappointment
- *pull one's weight* = do your fair share of the work
- *put on airs* = act superior
- *put on the back burner* = postpone
- *put the cart before the horse* = do things in the wrong order

R

- *red herring* = something that takes attention away from the real issue
- *red tape* = a lot of official rules, papers, details, that often prevent important things from getting done fast
- *roll up your sleeves* = get ready to work
- *runs a tight ship* = manages an organization in an orderly, disciplined manner

S

- *sleep on it* = think it over before making a decision
- *snow job* = an answer to a question that is full of nonsense and often flattery
- *spin one's wheels* = be in motion but get nowhere
- *split hairs* = make unimportant distinctions
- *straw that broke the camel's back* = the last thing, that when added to an already bad situation, causes failure
- *swan song* = last work produced by an artist, writer, or professional leaving a job
- *sweeten the pot* = make something even more attractive

ABOUT 100 IDIOMS AND THEIR MEANINGS (Continued)

T

- *take the bull by the horns* = deal with a problem head-on
- *talk turkey* = talk honestly and plainly about business or other practical matters
- *tell tales out of school* = reveal private or secret information
- *think on one's feet* = able to think and talk at the same time
- *threw me a curve* = confuse by doing something unexpected
- *tied up* = busy
- *tighten one's belt* = spend less money
- *tongue-in-cheek* = saying the opposite of what you really mean
- *too many irons in the fire* = too many different things to do at one time
- *tooth and nail* = with great determination
- *toot one's own horn* = brag, praise oneself
- *turn over a new leaf* = begin again; change some undesirable behavior

U

- *up a creek* = in a bad situation
- *up a tree* = in a bad situation and unable to get out of it

W

- *walk in someone else's shoes* = look at, experience something from another person's point of view
- *wet behind the ears* = young and inexperienced

"Ms. Barnes, isn't there *anyone* out there I can touch base with?"
(reprinted with permission of the author)

Do you know the meaning of the idiom "touch base"?

☞ ON YOUR WAY

Look and listen for idioms at work and in your home reading. When you find one in print:

a. Highlight or underline it.

b. Ask someone what it means.

c. Cut out the short article or paragraph in which it appears.

d. Tape it to an index card, write its meaning on the back of the card, and include it in your deck of new vocabulary words. Review your deck weekly.

S E C T I O N

III

BACK-UP SKILLS

cus´tom-er
re-place´ment
thank´ful
cham´pi-on
ap-pear´ance
de-light´ful
know´ledge
rev´e-nue
suc-ceed´
in´no-vate

The skills in this section are presented as a review of some of the basics of language.

SKILL 13: ON YOUR TERMS

Language-Experience Model

YOU are the most important element of the reading process! You bring to the printed word all that you are as a unique person: your knowledge, experiences, likes and dislikes, values, hopes, and successes.

Reading has everything to do with who you are and what you do, because reading is an **interaction between you and a printed text.**

Improving your reading requires:

- Knowing and valuing what you bring to the printed word.

- Learning how to use your knowledge and experience more effectively to meet your reading goals.

- Taking responsibility for your reading improvement.

Here is one way to begin:

Ask a friend, coworker, or trainer to help you complete the following procedure:

1. Choose a topic that interests you. Suggestions: a typical day in your life; what you like and don't like about your job; a biographical sketch, etc.

2. Dictate a short story about it to your reading assistant.

3. Ask your reading assistant to type and print the story.

4. Read the story back, asking for help, as needed.

Your reading assistant might also:

- Ask questions about the story you've dictated that prompt you to—

    —<u>Summarize</u> the main points.

    —<u>Recall</u> the details.

    —<u>Analyze</u> the ideas presented.

    —<u>Give</u> your personal <u>opinions</u>.

    —<u>Ask questions</u> of your own about the reading material.

    —<u>Relate</u> it to other areas of your work life.

Language-Experience Model (Continued)

- Put your story in another form—a chart, graph, or outline.
- Cut apart the individual words or phrases in your story, scramble them, and ask you to reorder them to make sense.
- Incorporate word recognition (SKILLS 10, 11, and 14) and phonics (SKILLS 17–19) exercises into your reading comprehension activities.
- Have you copy your story into a notebook.
- Ask you to generate more stories about your experiences to print and have you read back.
- Use other reading materials on subjects that interest you and are important to your job.

Your Turn! Tony dictated the following story to his reading assistant:

"I work at a fast food restaurant five days a week. I do a lot of different things there, depending on the day and how many people are working. Some days I do the same things all day, and on others, I do a variety of jobs.

I might clean tables, counters, and trays. I have to wipe off the cash register monitor screens and replace tray liners, too.

You have to move fast when you work in the kitchen, putting fries in the strainers and dipping them in the oil bins and compressing the burgers and buns. At peak times of the day, I wish I had six hands instead of two.

On days when I open the place, I've got to take all the supplies out of the boxes in the storage room and replace the paper rolls in the computer reader.

My favorite job is working the registers because I get to talk to customers."

THINK ABOUT, THEN DICTATE YOUR OWN PERSONAL ACCOUNT.

☞ **ON YOUR WAY**

To build your word recognition skills:

1. Cut out pictures from mail-order catalogs.

2. Paste them on index cards.

3. Practice saying the word you associate with each picture.

4. Write each word on the opposite side of each card.

Example: *Index card*

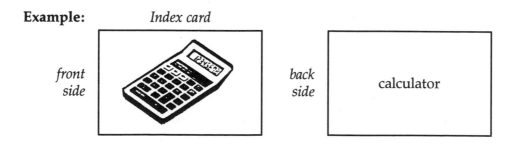

front side   *back side*   calculator

SKILL 14: BONDS

Occupational Word Families and Employment Language

Certain words appear repeatedly in **job ads** (advertisements) in the classified section of your newspaper.

Learning to read job ads correctly—to find the information you're looking for and respond to the ads appropriately—requires recognizing and learning the meanings of general words as well as the titles and technical terms that go with them.

There are many occupational families—or clusters of jobs—related to producing goods or providing services. They often share the same language or vocabulary. You can learn more about the occupations advertised below by looking in the *Dictionary of Occupational Titles,* found in the reference section of your library.

GENERAL VOCABULARY

- ☐ abilities
- ☐ accuracy
- ☐ administrative
- ☐ alternating
- ☐ applicants
- ☐ appointment
- ☐ appropriate
- ☐ aptitude
- ☐ assistant
- ☐ attitude
- ☐ available
- ☐ background
- ☐ career-minded
- ☐ certification
- ☐ challenging
- ☐ clerical
- ☐ commensurate
- ☐ communication skills
- ☐ competitive
- ☐ comprehensive
- ☐ conditions
- ☐ (in) confidence

CUSTOMER SERVICE ENTRY LEVEL

A leading manufacturer of laboratory equipment seeks an entry level person with strong mechanical aptitude to work in our customer service department..

Must have excellent communication skills and ability to interface effectively with customers, distributors and engineering. Fast-paced environment involving telephone contact. Customer service experience preferred. Send resume with salary requirements to:

**Data Processing
Data Coordinator**

In the busy Development Department of our northshore community hospital we have a full-time day opening for a computer experienced, detail-oriented, good communicator with excellent interpersonal, secretarial and accurate typing skills. At least 1 year of data processing coursework or training is required. While implementing/maintaining a computer-based record keeping system, you will generate & review daily/monthly summary reports of gift activity. A competitive salary and benefits package is offered. Send your resume or apply to:

CUSTOMER SERVICE/SALES REP

Qualified applicants must be highly motivated, outgoing and possess a minimum of 1+ years customer service and sales exp., along with PC data input skills and excellent oral/written interpersonal skills. Prior banking exp. is preferred.

We offer a competitive salary and an excellent benefit package. Please apply in person or send resume with salary history to:
Employment Manager

CUSTOMER RELATIONS

Machine Shop/Metal Working
$20–$30,000

Diversified administrative and office responsibilities. Must be familiar with metal working of machine shop environment, strong communication skills required. Apply with our management consultants at HRS/Human Resource.

CUSTOMER SERVICE SUPERVISOR

We have an excellent opportunity for an experienced Customer Service Supervisor to work in our fast-paced operation.

If you have a minimum of 3 yrs. supervisory experience in customer service and enjoy dealing with all types of people, please send your resume and current salary in confidence.

Customer Service Clerk

Mechanical service organization based in Oconomowoc is currently seeking a mechanically minded individual to perform clerical inventory, and shipping and receiving duties. Computerized inventory skills, typing and some accounting a plus. Forward resumes to:

CUSTOMER SERVICE/TELEMARKETING

Small manufacturing company seeking enthusiastic person who is detail oriented with good phone skills to work with customers nationwide. Must be self disciplined and highly motivated. Excellent company paid benefits, pleasant working conditions, nonsmoking office. Please send resume and salary requirements to:

Occupational Word Families (Continued)

- [ ] consideration
- [ ] convenient
- [ ] correspondence
- [ ] course
- [ ] courteous
- [ ] current
- [ ] customer
- [ ] decision-making
- [ ] degree
- [ ] departmental
- [ ] desirable
- [ ] detail-oriented
- [ ] enrolled
- [ ] enthusiastic
- [ ] entry level
- [ ] environment
- [ ] equivalent
- [ ] excellent
- [ ] exciting
- [ ] expanding
- [ ] experience
- [ ] exposure
- [ ] extensive
- [ ] facility
- [ ] familiarity
- [ ] fast-paced
- [ ] flexible
- [ ] goals
- [ ] graduate
- [ ] immediate
- [ ] implementing
- [ ] industry
- [ ] inquiries
- [ ] interested
- [ ] interpersonal
- [ ] knowledge

---

data processing
PROGRAMMER TRAINEE

National insurance statistical and advisory services organization has immediate need for recent business or math grad with PC programming training to provide microcomputer programming support. Knowledge of Basic, C, Paradox and COBOL highly desirable. Full range of employee benefits provided. Apply in confidence by sending resume to:

Data Entry
KEYPUNCH OPERATORS

Minimum requirements are at least 1 year of experience on Alpha & Numeric and a minimum of 12,000 key strokes (all candidates will be tested). Experience in UNIVAC 1900 systems preferred. CPU programming experience a plus. Heavy and mandatory overtime. We provide an excellent salary and benefits package. Please call for an appointment.

---

data processing
Peripheral Equipment Operator
2am to 10am

■ RUN IBM laser printers, check sorters and Bell-Howell Inserter operators. Must pass aptitude test and be flexible with work hours (occasional weekends required)

■ APPLICATIONS are taken in Personnel from 9am to Noon Monday thru Friday at Human Resources Dept.

Data Processing
SYSTEMS ANALYSTS

Our west suburban based firm is a leading provider of Forecasting/Inventory Mgmt. software serving IBM mainframes and DEC/VAX minis. We are seeking 2 SAs responsible for Application development/programming and automated software implementation.

Each position requires a minimum of 2 yrs. experience in either COBOL/MVS/CICS or VAX/VMS/FORTRAN (DBMS, TDMS, CDD a +). Degree or equivalent preferred. Good communication and analysis skills are essential.

Besides an excellent salary, we offer a full complement of benefits, pleasant working conditions and the opportunity to enhance your technical and business skills. Please reply via letter or resume to:

DIR MIS

Banking
OPERATIONS

Medium size branch of major international foreign bank seeks a bright, organized person with familiarity on personal computers to handle wire transfers/loans to processing transactions. Typing ability with exposure on domestic and internat'l wire transfers ideal. We offer good startup salary and benefits. Please call our H.R. Recruiter for appt.

BANKING
TELLERS

Near N. side bank seeks career-minded, full time expd. Universal Tellers. A min. of 1 year exp. required. NCR exp. helpful. Must be willing to work at any of our 5 facilities in N. side area. Good figure aptitude and excellent customer service skills nec.

Excellent salary, benefits, and transportation. Apply in person to:

Banking
TELLER SUPERVISOR

Excellent opportunity for an individual who possesses a minimum of one year supervisory or head teller experience. The successful candidate will be self-motivated, derive satisfaction from achieving results and be committed to quality customer service. The candidate will have an active role in scheduling, establishing standards, completing performance evaluations, training new hires and interacting with our customer base. We offer a competitive salary based on qualifications and comprehensive benefits, including profit sharing. For consideration, forward your resume and salary history to:

MORTGAGE LOAN COUNSELOR

One of the nation's leading mortgage bankers is seeking several individuals to join our expanding staff.

Hired individuals will be responsible for a portfolio of delinquent accounts which requires a high level of decision making ability, extensive telephone contact, and CRT work.

Candidates must possess excellent communication skills and the ability to counsel people regarding financial problems. Previous experience in customer service, collections, or telemarketing is helpful.

We offer our employees a competitive salary and benefit package as well as an excellent internal promotion program. If you meet our requirements and are interested in a growing company, submit resume or call Monday–Thursday 10:00 a.m.–noon.

Insurance
GENERAL CLERK

Progressive insurance company is seeking a detail-oriented, entry-level general clerk to support its Statistical Department. Duties include balancing and distributing underwriter profitability reports; monitoring state insurance department reports; light typing of correspondence; key-fasting and assisting in other departmental responsibilities. Qualifications include high school diploma, good figure aptitude; property and casualty insurance experience preferred, knowledge of CRT and PC desirable but willing to train. This position offers the opportunity for cross-training into a technical position. We offer competitive benefits including: ESOP, 401(K), paid vacations and holiday. Annual salary is in the $14,000-$16,000 range. Interested candidates please send resume to:

Insurance
SERVICE REPRESENTATIVE

We have a position for a service rep with experience in billing, coverage & health claims. Duties include heavy phone contact and correspondence. Qualified individuals must possess exc. communication skills, CRT, & the ability to work in a fast paced environment.

In return, we offer you a salary commensurate with experience and a congenial work environment. For consideration, please submit resume with salary to:

Insurance
CLAIM TRAINEES
CLAIM REPS

Our Regional Service Office has immediate opportunities available in the growing and aggressive Property & Casualty Insurance subsidiary of the largest insurer.

These positions in our Claims Department are ideal for individuals with college degrees. Applicants must have excellent written and oral communication skills, demonstrated leadership ability and a proven academic background. We will also consider candidates who have 1–2 years of property and casualty claim handling experience. For our trainee positions, we would like to see 1–2 years of work experience in a customer service environment.

In addition to the professional working conditions expected from an industry leader, we will provide you with complete training, a competitive starting salary and a liberally structured benefits package.

Please forward a letter outlining your career goals and interests along with your resume to:

Human Resource Department

- [ ] located
- [ ] maintaining
- [ ] mandatory
- [ ] mathematical
- [ ] minimum
- [ ] motivated
- [ ] necessary
- [ ] opening
- [ ] opportunity
- [ ] oral
- [ ] organizational skills
- [ ] outgoing
- [ ] outstanding
- [ ] possess
- [ ] preferred
- [ ] prior
- [ ] professional
- [ ] progressive
- [ ] qualifications
- [ ] requirements
- [ ] responsible
- [ ] resume
- [ ] rewarding
- [ ] salary history
- [ ] schedule
- [ ] secretarial
- [ ] self-disciplined
- [ ] skills
- [ ] specialist
- [ ] submit
- [ ] successful
- [ ] weekends

ACCOUNTS PAYABLE

No work experience or returning to the work force after an absence so employment doors are slow to open? If this is your situation but you are responsible, have an eager to learn attitude, and work well in a true team environment, we are willing to train. Position is available in the Accounts Payable Dept of a national health care firm. Responsibilities include invoice processing, account coding, and telephone inquiry. Job requires accuracy, attention to detail, organizational abilities, and ten key calculator skills. Send resume and salary requirements to:

PAYROLL SPECIALIST

National payroll firm needs payroll specialist in our field office. Qualifications should include: good math aptitude, computer keyboard experience and excellent customer service skills. Payroll experience helpful. Excellent career opportunity in a growing company. Call 782-8123 or send resume directly to:

Accounting
CONTROLLER

We are a service corporation heavily involved in the field of finance. We have an immediate need for a professional with at least 2 years experience that is well organized, has a background in public accounting and is conversant with personal computers. This is an opportunity for you to help build an expanding small company. You will have total responsibility for all accounting work in the company.

We are conveniently located near the Northwestern station and offer competitive compensation package and comprehensive benefits.

Please send a resume or write with salary history included to:

Retail
DISPLAY TECHNICIAN

We have career opportunities in our Chicago area stores. Individuals for these positions must have own car.

Fashion knowledge and previous visual presentation experience, preferably in womens specialty stores. High school education with art background helpful. Good physical condition, able to climb ladder and moderate lifting.

Interested applicants should call Susan Barney at:

Retail
ASSISTANT STORE MANAGER
Merchandising

Is currently interviewing at our State Street location for a self-motivated individual to achieve planned sales goals; oversee merchandising; motivate/develop staff; and guarantee quality customer satisfaction.

Requirements include:

- [ ] 2 years experience as an Assistant Store Manager-Merchandising in a high volume department store
  OR
- [ ] 2 years experience as a district manager in a specialty store environment
- [ ] A strong ability and desire to motivate others
- [ ] Proven analytical skills to track and increase sales
- [ ] Buying experience preferred

We offer an excellent salary, competitive benefits package and a generous store-wide discount. If you feel your qualifications meet our needs, please forward your resume and salary history in confidence to:

OPERATING ROOM TECHNICIANS

Hospital is seeking full and part time operating room technicians to help expand their current surgery area. Hospital is a large hospital, with 5 operating suites expanding to 6 suites. We offer a variety of procedures, a clinical ladder to develop your professional career and a team of professionals to work with in a challenging and rewarding environment. If you're an experienced ORT or a new graduate looking for an exciting opportunity, please contact

PERSONNEL DEPARTMENT

health care
PATIENT CASE SPECIALIST

Patients are of vital importance to Hospitals. If people are your specialty, join us in the management of the admission, in-house support, discharge & post-discharge and follow-up of patients admitted to the Hospitals.

Requires 2+ years within a hospital finance area. Knowledge of, and ability to interpret and apply complex policies regarding admissions, state and third party payor (insurance) regulations is expected. Strong interpersonal skills including tact, discretion and courtesy are a must; analytical skills and problem solving abilities are essential. BA degree or the equivalent is required.

A competitive salary complete with full benefits will be offered. For consideration, send your resume to:

Health Care
MEDICAL TECHNOLOGISTS

A leader in the clinical laboratory field located just west of O'Hare Airport near Elk Grove Village, is accepting applications for positions in their laboratory.

To qualify, you must have the appropriate degree and certification. Positions are available in the following Depts:

- Blood Bank (Nights)
- Serology; Part-Time (Days)
- Toxicology

We offer excellent benefits including dental, vision and health insurance plus HMO, paid lunch hour, 401K, hospital days, free days plus a day for your birthday, tuition reimbursement, pay for unused sick time, and 3 weeks vacation after 2 years.

To take advantage of these opportunities and learn more about your future, please respond to:

Health Care
SUPERVISOR HOUSEKEEPING

Full time supervisor of Environmental Services at our 325-bed community hospital. Will inspect all check outs, train staff and review procedures, plus prepare daily reports. Must have prior supervisory experience and understanding of institutional housekeeping procedures. Must have knowledge of supplies and equipment. Excellent salary commensurate with experience plus outstanding benefits package. Send resume with salary requirements to:

Insurance
UNDERWRITER
D&O Liability

Join This World Leader At Our Newly Opened Office in Cleveland

Underwriting managers affiliated with the Surety Company, is opening a branch office in Cleveland. We currently seek a professional with the judgement and decision-making skills to underwrite premiums for Directors and Officers liability insurance.

Your minimum of 3+ years' related business experience must be complemented by at least one year of D&O underwriting. Strong analytical and communication skills are essential; and since this is a field position covering a wide area, you must have the flexibility to travel and handle overtime as necessary. An initial training program will take place in our Hartford, CT area headquarters.

We offer a generous compensation package and opportunities for continued advancement. For consideration, please send your resume in confidence to:

Occupational Word Families (Continued)

retail sales
FRONT DESK MANAGER

Your top performance, friendly, team spirited personality and ambition are what we are looking for at our exclusive high fashion retail store. You will greet customers, write orders and wear many other hats. Your sense of presence, figure aptitude and efficiency are key. Good salary & benefits. Please send your resume to:

MEDICATION ASSISTANT

If you are enrolled in a 2 or 4 year Nursing Program and have had a Pharmacology course you may be eligible to work as a Medication Assistant in our long term health care facility.

We offer a competitive wage and benefit package to include on-site child care at $9/day and 401K Plan. If interested, please call:

Your Turn! 1. Please read the words on the **GENERAL VOCABULARY** list. Then read the job ads on each page. Every time you meet a word in a job ad that is on the word list, highlight (or underline) it in the job ad and put a check mark next to the word on the list.

Your Turn! 2. Please choose one job ad that interests you on each of the previous pages. After reading each ad, enter the information given in the ad in the appropriate columns:

Job Title	Required Skills	Required Experience	Required Personal Traits	Technical Terms I Need To Know

Repeat this exercise every time you prepare to answer a job ad. It will help you match your knowledge and skills with the job requirements stated in the ad.

Alphabetical Order

You know that the English alphabet follows a certain order called **alphabetical order** (or **alpha order**).

You know the alphabet and probably use alphabetical order daily to find information in data bases, directories, manuals, maps, and reference materials of all kinds.

Let's face it! We haven't found a better way to arrange volumes of information that anyone knowing our language can access—and we probably won't.

If you learn to use alphabetical order skillfully, you'll be able to do your job faster and with fewer errors.

> • <u>Some</u> <u>basic</u> <u>tips</u>   and   • <u>Lots</u> <u>of</u> <u>practice</u>

<u>will</u> <u>help</u> <u>you</u> <u>develop</u> <u>this</u> <u>critical</u> <u>skill.</u>

Think of the alphabet in sections:

1	A	B	C	D	E	F	G
2			H	I	J	K	
3		L	M	N	O	P	
4		Q	R	S	T	U	V
5			W	X	Y	Z	

Picture these sections in your mind when you're filing or searching for a file on your terminal, or looking for a company in a directory, a word in the dictionary, or street name on a map.

Practicing putting words in alphabetical order (alphabetizing) will help you remember how to find quickly any word you're looking for.

HOW TO BEGIN   Look at the *first letter* of each of the words you're working with. If the words begin with *different* letters, arrange the words in alphabetical order *according to their first letters.*

Alphabetical Order

Example: | r |educers   1. | d |uotone

            | d |uotone   2. | e |tch

            | w |eb   3. | o |ffset

            | e |tch   4. | r |educers

            | o |ffset   5. | w |eb

Alphabetical Order (Continued)

HOW TO CONTINUE If all the words begin with the *same* letter, look at the **second** letter of each of the words. If the second letters are all different, arrange the words in alphabetical order according to the second letters.

	Alphabetical Order
Example: g u mming	1. g a lley
g a lley	2. g e neration
g r ain	3. g o ldenrod
g e neration	4. g r ain
g o ldenrod	5. g u mming

If all the words begin with the *same two* letters, arrange them in alphabetical order according to their **third** letters.

	Alphabetical Order
Example: fo n t	1. fo c al
fo g	2. fo g
fo l io	3. fo l io
fo r mat	4. fo n t
fo c al	5. fo r mat

If all the words begin with the *same three* letters, arrange them in order according to their **fourth** letters.

	Alphabetical Order
Example: con s istent	1. con c ealed
con i ferous	2. con d ensed
con c ealed	3. con i ferous
con t act	4. con s istent
con d ensed	5. con t act

AND SO ON...

Your Turn! **1.** Please complete this statement after examining the words below. Then put them in alphabetical order.

If all the words begin with the same _____ letters, arrange them in order according to their _____ letters.

concealing	1. _____
concealer	2. _____
concealment	3. _____
concealable	4. _____

ANSWERS: seven, eighth 1. concealable 2. concealer 3. concealing 4. concealment

Your Turn!

2. Your computer system is ''down,'' which means you'll have to alphabetize these files manually. See how fast and accurately you can do it.

Rodgers, Katherina L.

Robinson, Gina M.

Rodriguez, Hector A.

Robbins, Michael J.

Roberts, Jeremy S.

Robberstein, David H.

Roberts, Jeffrey P.

Robertson, Tricia J.

Rodriguez, Hector R.

Rogers, Sarah T.

Robin, Anthony

Hint: *Separate (and alphabetize) the names in groups before rearranging them in alphabetical order.*

Example: —Names beginning with ''Robb''

—Names beginning with ''Robert''

—Names beginning with ''Robi''

—Names beginning with ''Rod,'' *and so on . . .*

WORKSPACE

1. _____

2. _____

3. _____

4. _____

5. _____

6. _____

7. _____

8. _____

9. _____

10. _____

11. _____

ANSWERS: 1. Robberstein, David H. 2. Robbins, Michael J. 3. Roberts, Jeffrey P. 4. Roberts, Jeremy S. 5. Robertson, Tricia K. 6. Robin, Anthony 7. Robinson, Gina M. 8. Rodgers, Katherina L. 9. Rodriguez, Hector A. 10. Rodriguez, Hector R. 11. Rogers, Sarah T.

SKILL 16: POWERHOUSE, POWER TOOL

The Dictionary

15 Ways a Dictionary Can *Energize* Your Reading

☑ **Guide Words**
(1st & last words on
a page)

→ sinister/siren

☑ **Word Meanings**
(definitions)
Read all the meanings
given. Then choose the
most suitable one for
your use.

☑ **Pronunciations**

☑ **Syllabication**
(division of words into
syllables or parts)

☑ **Accents**

☑ **Spelling**
(+ verb and adjective
forms, plurals)

☑ **Word Origins**
(etymologies)

☑ **Parts of Speech**

☑ **Synonyms**
(See SKILL 21)

☑ **Idioms**

☑ **Capitalization**

☑ **Usage Labels**

☑ **Subject Labels**

☑ **Illustrations**

☑ **Mythology**

sin-is-ter (sin'i stər) *adj.* [< L. *sinister*, left hand] 1. threatening harm, evil, or trouble 2. bad, wicked, evil 3. *orig.*, of or on the left side
SYN. base, disastrous, foretelling danger

sink (singk) *vi.* [OE. *sincan*] 1. to fall downward slowly 2. to become partly or completely submerged in water 3. to become lower or weaker in value 4. to appear to go down, as the sun 5. to pass gradually into a less active state (sleep, ill-health, etc.) *vt.* 1. to cause to fall, make go down, under, lower, or weaker 2. to dig a well 3. to send (a ball) into a hole or pocket in golf, billiards, basketball, etc. 4. to invest money *n.* 1. a basin with a drainpipe 2. a cesspool or sewer 3. *Printing* the extra space left at the top of the page for the beginnings of a chapter, etc. ___ *Idiom* *sink or swim.* to fail or succeed, depending on one's own efforts

sink-er (sing'kər) *n.* 1. a person or thing that sinks 2. a weight used to sink a fishing line 3. [Colloq.] a doughnut

sinking fund a fund used to extinguish a debt

Sino- [< LGk. *Sinai*] a combining form, meaning Chinese and . . .(such as Sino-Japanese meaning Chinese and Japanese)

sin-u-ate (sin'yoo āt) *adj.* [< L. *sinuatus*, bent, curved] 1. winding; bent in and out 2. *Bot.* having a wavy margin, like some leaves

Sioux (soo) *n., pl.* Sioux (soo, sooz) [< Fr., short for *Nadowessioux* < Ojibwa *Nadoweisiu* enemy, lit. little snake] a member of any of various American Indian peoples, esp. of the Dakota tribe *adj.* pertaining to this tribe.

sire (sīr) *n.* [< L. *senior*, *comp.* of *senex*, old] 1. a father or ancestor 2. title of respect used to address a sovereign or king 3. *Archaic* an important person, or one in a position of authority
sir-ee (sə rē') *interj.,* often used with no or yes

si-ren (sī'rən) *n.* [< Gr. *Seiren*] 1. *Gr. & Roman Myth.* any one of a group of sea nymphs, represented as part bird and part woman, that used their singing to lure sailors to their destruction 2. a seductive woman 3. a whistle or similar device used as a warning signal

Your Turn! Find the answers to each of these questions on the sample dictionary page to the right. Draw lines to your choices and then write them on the lines provided.

1. A word taken directly from the French

   _____

2. Plural form of **panoply**

   _____

3. A word used in anatomy and zoology

   _____

4. Two synonyms for **panic**

   _____

5. A Greek prefix meaning ''all''

   _____

6. Etymology of **pantry** and **panocha**

   _____

7. A character in Greek mythology

   _____

8. One word having two different and separately-entered meanings

   _____

9. A word that can be pronounced two ways

   _____

10. A word created by an English poet

    _____

11. A word spelled differently when used as a noun, adjective, and verb (some forms)

    _____

pan-a-cea (pan'ə se'ə) *n.* [< Gr. *pan*, all + *akeisthai*, to cure] a supposed cure-all, or remedy for all things

pa-nache (pə nash', pə näsh') *n.* [< Fr. *panache*, ult. < L. *penna*, a feather] 1. an ornamental plume, esp. on a helmet 2. a flamboyant, spirited manner; an elegant style

pan-cre-as (pan'kre əs, pang'-) *n.* *Anat.Zool.* [< Gr. *pan*, all + *kreas*, flesh] a large gland, located near the stomach, that secretes a digestive juice into the intestines and insulin into the blood

Pan-do-ra (pan dôr'ə) [< Gr. *pan*, all + *doron*, gift] *Gr. Myth.* the first woman, created by the gods to punish mankind for stealing fire: she opened a box that set free all human ills into the world

pan-han-dle (pan'han'd'l) *n.* a narrow strip of land projecting like the handle of a pan

pan-han-dle (pan'han'd'l) *vt., vi.* -dled, -dling [Colloq.] to beg from passers-by on the street

pan-ic (pan'ik) *n.* [< Gr. *panikos*, of Pan (because he was said to have caused sudden fear in crowds and herds)] a sudden, unreasonable fear, often spreading quickly *vt.* -icked, -icking 1. terrify or cause to lose self-control and flee 2. [Slang] to highly amuse an audience *adj.* panicky *SYN.* fear, alarm, terror, dread, fright

pa-no-cha (pə nō'chə) *n.* [Am.Sp., ult.< L. *panis*, bread] a dark, coarse grade of Mexican sugar, *var.* of penuche

pan-o-ply (pan'ə plē) *n., pl.* -plies [< Gr. *pan*- all + *hopla*, arms] 1. a complete suit of armor 2. any splendid array, or complete equipment or covering

pan-to-graph (pan'tə graf') *n.* 1. an instrument that mechanically copies diagrams, plans, etc. 2. *Elect.* an insulated framework for conveying electric current from overhead wires to motors

ANSWERS: 1. panache 2. panoplies 3. panacea/pantry 4. pancreas 5. fear, alarm, etc. 6. pan 7. Latin, panis, bread 8. Pandora 9. panhandle 10. panache, pancreas 11. pandemonium 12. panic

SKILL 17: CO-WORKERS

Consonant Blends

Consonant blends are combinations of two or three consonants, each with a distinct sound, that go together—blend smoothly with the other(s).

> Examples: **bl, cl, fl, gl, pl, sl, br, cr, dr, fr, gr, pr, tr, spr**

Digraphs are combinations of two consonants that produce a totally different sound than either of the consonants makes separately.

> Examples: **ch**—**ch**ew/**ch**orus/**ch**ef   **ng**—si**ng**
> **th**—**th**in, **th**an   **sh**—**sh**oe
> **ph**—**ph**oto
> **wh**—**wh**ite

Consonant blends and digraphs have been paired with vowels and end blends to generate the lists of word families below. Each blend/digraph is in dark or **boldface** print.

Mastering the correct sounding or pronunciation of these words—and their recognition—is a big step forward in reading skill development.

black	**bl**ank	**bl**inker
clack	**cl**ank	**cl**ink
flack	**fl**ank	**sl**ink
slack	**pl**ank	**br**ink
crackers	**cr**ank	**dr**ink
track	**dr**ank	**tr**inket
smack	**fr**ank	**st**ink
stack	**pr**ank	**shr**inking
shack	**sh**ank	**th**ink
whack	**sp**ank	
	stank	
	swanky	
	shrank	
block	**th**ankful	**bl**imp
clock		**cr**imped
flock		**pr**imp
crock		**sk**imp
frock		**scr**imp
smock		**shr**imp
stock		**ch**imp
shocked		
sprocket		

bland	blush	blend	brilliant
clan	flush	trend	drill
gland	plush	slender	frill
slander	slush	spend	trill
brand	brush	splendor	skills
grand	crushed		spill
spandex	thrush		still
stand			shrill
strand			thriller
			chilly

blow	clamp	clash	cling
flow	cramp	flash	fling
glowing	tramp	slash	sling
slow	scamp	brash	bring
crow	stamp	crash	sting
showy	champion	trash	swinging
throw		smash	spring
		stash	string
		splash	thing
		thrash	

clump	clunk	click	flint
plumper	flunk	flick	glint
slump	plunk	slick	printer
crumple	drunk	prick	stint
grumpy	trunk	trick	splint
trump	skunk	sticker	
stump	spunk	stricken	
thump	stunk	chicken	
chump	shrunk	thick	
	chunk		

blot	clap	brat

Your Turn! See how many words you can generate that rhyme (sound the same as) with ''blot,'' ''clap,'' and ''brat,'' and begin with the consonant blends and digraphs you worked with in the word families above.

ANSWERS: clot, plot, slot, spot, shot, Scott, (throttle)
slap, crap, trap, strap, chap, flat, slat, stat, spat, chat, (platter)

SKILL 18: SINGLES AND DOUBLES

Vowel Matching

(Sometimes vowels "work" alone to create a sound; other times they "double up" to create the sound.) Although the English language is confusing at times, looking for letter/sound patterns in the words you read can make mastering it a lot easier. The following lists will give you a start.

Practice saying the lists out loud. Then read them again silently, noting the ways in which the words in each list are the same and yet different.

ate	ace	lemonade	bake	ale
create	face	faded	cake	bale
locate	lace	made	fake	dale
elaborate	mace	waders	Lakers	male
enunciate	pace	blade	remake	pale
lubricate	racer	glade	rake	resale
date	brace	grade	forsaken	tale
intimidate	embrace	degrade	take	scale
inundate	place	trade	wake	stale
fate	replacement	spade	cornflake	
gate	displace		brake	
congregate	trace		drake	
irrigate	space		snakeskin	
delegate			stake	
hate			earthquake	
late				
collate				
innoculate				
relate	became	caper		
translate	dame	gape		
mate	fame	nape		
primate	gamesman	rape		
rate	lame	tape		
berate	nickname	drape		
crate	same	grape		
grateful	tamer	escape		
plate	blamed	landscape		
template	flame	scapegoat		
slate	frame	scrape		
skater	mainframe			
statement				

Can you name two things all of these words have in common?

They all have a long a and a silent e.

bay	ail	dice	beach
day	bail	ice	each
today	Braille	lice	impeach
Tuesday	fail	mice	reach
gay	hail	rice	teacher
hay	jail	entice	bleach
bluejay	mailman	advice	breach
okay	pail	slice	preached
relay	guardrail	spicy	
may	railroad	price	
nay	derail	splice	
prepayment	sailor	thrice	beak
x-ray	detail		leaking
say	tailor		peak
midway	prevail		teak
clay	flail	fight	weaken
display	trail	knight	bleak
slaying	entrails	delightful	freak
mainstay	trailer	might	speaker
crayfish		night	sneakers
stray		self-righteous	streaked
gray		unsightly	squeak
praying	laid	tight	
spray	maid	blight	
tray	braid	flights	
betrayal	afraid	plight	deal
sway		slight	healing
		brightest	meal
		frightening	Neal
	Cain		repeal
	disdain		really
	regain		sealant
	mainstream	bide	teal
	painful	decide	veal
	plain	insecticide	zeal
	plaintiff	suicide	steal
	containment	confided	squeal
	vain	guide	
	brain	hide	
	drain	ride	
	refrain	aside	
	ingrain	outsider	
	trainee	yuletide	
	sprained	widening	
	restraining	bride	
	obtain	unbridled	
		pride	
		gliders	
		slide	
	maim		
	claim		

Middle column (bite group): bite, kite, mite, rite, site, smite, despite, sprite, trite, white, quite

Vowel Matching (Continued)

beam	offbeat	boat	boon	boil
ream	feature	coat	baboon	recoil
seam	heat	goat	cocoon	foil
team	meat	moat	goon	soiled
creamed	neatly	bloated	loon	toilet
dream	beneath	floating	balloon	broil
steam	repeat	gloat	bassoon	spoil
streamers	seat		buffoon	voille
screaming	bleat		saloon	
	cleats	coach	maroon	
	pleat	poached	platoon	coin
bean	treatment	encroach	spoon	sirloin
dean		reproach		groin
jeans				
meaningful	beaver		food	
wean	leave	boast	mood	
cleaners	weave	coast	brood	
	bereaved	roast		
		toaster		
dear			book	
fearful	deadly		precooked	
gear	headline	goad	cookie	
hear	read	reload	hook	
nearby	bread	roadblock	looked	
appearance	dreadful	toad	nook	
rear	instead		undertook	
arrears	treadmill		brook	
bleary	spread	boyfriend	crook	
clearly	thread	coy	shook	
dreary		annoyed		
smear		deploy		
shear	believe	Roy		
	grievance	soybean		
	relieve	destroyed		
cease	retrieve			
deceased	achieved			
lease				
release				
decreasing	niece			
increase	piecemeal			
	grief			
	priest			

Your Turn!

This blurb appeared in a small corner of a company newsletter. But the typesetter had omitted the same letter in all of the words with a blank space.

Which of the typesetter's keys wasn't working properly?

> Cel__ste was a gu__st at the B__st W__stern. L__st you think she was there to r__st, I can att__st to the fact that she went, with z__st, at the requ__st of her boss, to answer qu__stions and dig__st sugg__stions regarding the new inv__stments in which her company was inter__sted.

Notice how easily you decoded this sentence. Why wasn't it a problem?

What have you learned about your ability to supply information that's not on a page?

ANSWER: e

SKILL 19: THE SILENT TREATMENT

Silent Letters

The letter ''e'' at the end of a word is almost never pronounced.

Examples: instance   like   measure   route

There are other letters that don't make a sound when combined with other letters in certain words. When you meet the words below in your reading, or say them, give the crossed-out letters ''the silent treatment.''

abscess	bridge	christen
conscious	ridge	fasten
fascination	dodge	glisten
muscle	lodge	listen
reminisce	fudge	
scene	judge	
science	nudge	calf
		half
acquaint	balk	
adjacent	caulk	chassis
adjourn	chaulk	
adjust	stalk	
	talk	climb
		comb
aghast		plumbing
ghost	biscuit	thumb
	circuit	
alms		clique
balm	bruise	critique
calm	juice	picturesque
psalm	nuisance	statuesque
qualm		
salmon		
salve	business	clothes
badge	bustle	colonel
hedge	hustle	
knowledge	castle	
ledge	mistletoe	debt
pledge	thistle	doubt
wedge	whistle	subtle
	wrestle	

depot

diaphragm
paradigm

diarrhea
hemorrhage

exhibit

fatigue
fugue
league
colleague
tongue
vague
vogue
folk
Polk
yolk

gnarl
gnash
gnat
gnaw
gnome
gnu

guarantee
guard
guess
guest
guide
guilty
guitar

herb

hymn
column
solemn

Illinois

knack
knapsack
knead
knee
kneel
knew
knife
knight
knit
knob
knock
knot
know
knuckle

lacquer
placque
technique
unique

mortgage
rapport
often

pneumonia
psalm

receipt

rhinoceros

schism
scissors

thyme

toward

vehicle

victuals

whole

wreck
wring
wrist
write
written
wrote
wrong

SKILL 20: BEFORES AND AFTERS

Prefixes and Suffixes

Prefix = one or more letters placed in **front of a word** to form a new word

You're already familiar with prefixes and how they work. You know that:

> **re**discover = to discover **again**
> **un**official = **not** official
> **mis**judge = to judge **wrongly**
> **trans**port = to carry **over** or **across**

Knowing prefixes can help you figure out the meanings of words that might look new to you. It's like having a set of keys to unlock the meanings of new words.

Once you know that the Greek prefix **"hyper-"** means **"over,"** or **"above normal,"** for example, you can more easily figure out the meanings of these words:

> **hyper**active = **over** active
> **hyper**critical = **over** critical
> **hyper**thermia = **over**heated; **above normal** fever
> +

hundreds of other words in the English language that begin with **"hyper."**

Here are more keys to add to your set:

PREFIX	MEANINGS	EXAMPLES
• **a-, an** =	**not, without**	• **a**typical = **not** typical *It was atypical of the group she belonged to.*
		• **an**hydrous = **without** water *The chemist worked with an anhydrous solution.*
• **ab-, a-** =	**from, away**	• **ab**olish = do **away** with *They abolished the outdated procedure.*
		• **a**vert = turn **away,** ward off *The disaster could not be averted.*
• **ad-** =	**to, towards, near**	• **ad**here = stick **to** *Please adhere to this company policy.*
		• **ad**dendum = something added **to** *The addendum helped explain the report.*

PREFIX	MEANINGS	EXAMPLES
• co-, col-, com-, con-, cor-=	with, together	• **co**insurance = insurance **with** two companies *Please notify the Benefits Department if you have coinsurance.* • **col**laborate = work **together** *Let's collaborate on the JIT project.* • **con**solidation = bringing **together** *Consolidation of the work units will increase our efficiency.* • **cor**relate = relate **with** *The statistics don't correlate.*
• de-=	from, down	• **de**mote = move **down** *We will have to demote you unless your error ratio improves.* • **de**regulate = take restrictions **from** *Competition among the airlines has increased since the government deregulated that industry.*
• dis-, dif-=	away, apart, opposite of, different	• **dis**engage = take **away** or release from something that holds or connects *Disengage the parts before passing them to your coworker.* • **dis**crepancy = **difference** *Your report contains several glaring discrepancies.*
• ex-, e-, ec-=	out, from, away	• **ex**cise = cut **out** *The surgeon excised the tumor with ease.* • **e**rode = wear **away** *Constant criticism can erode self-confidence.* • **ec**centric = away **from** the center *Though his mannerisms were eccentric, his work was commendable.*
• in-, im-, =	into	• **in**corporate = bring **into** *Incorporate the results of your research into your report.* • **im**plement = bring **into** use *The firm implemented a new retirement program.*
• in-, il-, im-, ir-=	not	• **in**ept = **not** apt, unfit *Though his credentials were glowing, his work proved inept.* • **ir**revocable = **not** able to be retracted or revoked *The decision to shut down the plant was irrevocable.*
• inter-=	between	• **inter**departmental = **between** departments *Interdepartmental communication was businesslike but friendly.*

Prefixes and Suffixes (Continued)

PREFIX	MEANINGS	EXAMPLES

- **infra-** =   beneath   • **infra**structure = **beneath** the structure
  The organization's infrastructure was crumbling.

- **intra-** =   within   • **intra**cardiac = **within** the heart   *An intracardiac catheter was used during the exam.*

- **per-** =   through, completely   • **per**forate = make a hole **through**
  The perforations in the pages of the handbooks made them easy to remove.

  - • **Per**use = read carefully, **completely**   *Peruse the instructions manual before operating the machine.*

- **pre-** =   before   • **pre**cooked = cooked **before,** ahead of time
  Dinner could be served in 15 minutes because the ham was precooked.

  - • **pre**empt = take **before** or ahead of
  The customer service seminar preempted our switchboard duties.

- **syn-, sym-** =   with, together   • **syn**drome = signs or symptoms occurring **together**   *A tardiness syndrome was developing in the warehouse.*

  - • **sym**biotic = living **with,** closely knit
  A symbiotic relationship existed between the parent company and its subsidiaries.

Your Turn! Match the words and meanings that follow.

____	1. **de**flect	a.	**not** reasonable
____	2. **ad**jacent	b.	lasting **through** the years
____	3. **in**tangible	c.	conspiring **with** someone in a scheme
____	4. **col**lusion	d.	bring something new **into** an environment
____	5. **ab**errant	e.	wandering **away** from the normal course
____	6. **intra**venous	f.	a meeting **with** others to discuss a particular subject
____	7. **ex**hale	g.	**not** able to be touched
____	8. **ir**rational	h.	**opposite** of ''to pay attention to''
____	9. **dis**regard	i.	**within** the veins
____	10. **pre**determine	j.	breathe **out**
____	11. **per**ennial	k.	lying **near**
____	12. **ab**solve	l.	bend **down;** turn **from** a straight direction
____	13. **sym**posium	m.	free **from** blame
____	14. **in**novate	n.	decide **before**

ANSWERS: 1. l   2. k   3. g   4. c   5. e   6. i   7. j   8. a   9. h   10. n   11. b   12. m   13. f   14. d

Suffix = one or more letters placed at the **end of a word** that add to or change the
meaning of the word

You're probably familiar with suffixes and how they work. You know that:

cheer**ful** = **full** of cheer
color**less** = **without** color
counsel**or** = **one who** counsels or advises

Just like a prefix, each suffix has a meaning.

Knowing suffixes gives you another set of keys to unlock the meanings of new
words—and the ways these words are used in sentences. Once you know that the
suffix **"-ize"** means **"to make,"** for example, you can more easily figure out the
meanings of these words:

standard**ize** = **to make** standard or uniform
verbal**ize** = **to make** verbal, use words to express
trauma**tize** = **to create** trauma, to injure

+

dozens of other words ending in **"-ize"** that are continually used to make our
language more efficient.

Here are some useful suffix keys to add to your set:

SUFFIX	MEANINGS	EXAMPLES
• **-able, -ible** =	**able, can**	• retriev**able** = **able** to bring back or retrieve
		• flex**ible** = **able** to bend
		• recogniz**able** = **able** to recognize or see
• **-ate** =	**to cause, make**	• evacu**ate** = **to make** vacant, empty
		• alien**ate** – **to cause** to be alien or alone
• **-esce** =	**to become, begin, grow**	• adol**escent** = **becoming** an adult
		• obsol**escent** = **becoming** obsolete, outdated
		• acqui**esce** = **to grow** silent, accept without protest
• **-ion, -sion, -tion** =	**act of, state of, result of**	• rebell**ion** = **act of** rebelling
		• condens**ation** = **state of** being condensed
		• revi**sion** = **result of** revising, correcting

Prefixes and Suffixes (Continued)

SUFFIX	MEANINGS	EXAMPLES
-ify =	to make	simplify = **to make** simple
		rectify = **to make** right
		nullify = **to make** void
		amplify = **to make** larger or greater
-ist, -yst =	person who	machinist = **person who** works with machines
		analyst = **person who** analyzes or studies data
-ment =	state of being	achievement = **state of being** achieved or accomplished
		alignment = **state of being** in a straight line
-ology =	study, science of	oncology = the **study of** tumors
		geology = earth **science**
		geneology = the **study of** one's origins or ancestry
-ous =	full of	porous = **full of** pores
		pretentious = **full of** pretense, false claims
		judicious = **full of** good judgment

Your Turn! Use the suffixes above to form words suggested by the phrases in the parentheses.

Four people were seeking **a.** _____ (state of being employed) as head of Prescott's fine jewelry department. While all four were **b.** _____ (able to be relied on) and **c.** _____ (full of industry), two had taken courses in **d.** _____ (study of precious gems) at the local vocational school. The position **e.** _____ (made necessary) being interviewed by both the head of the Human Resources Department and the store manager. A personnel assistant had **f.** _____ (made simple) the hiring process by having the candidates complete written **g.** _____ (act of applying) in advance. Before the four job-seekers left Prescott's, they were told they'd be **h.** _____ (made known) within 10 days, of the store's decision.

SKILL 21: SAMES, OPPOSITES, SOUNDS-THE-SAME, LOOKS-THE-SAME

Synonyms, Antonyms, Homophones, Homographs

SYNONYMS = words that have the **same** (or almost the same) meaning(s)

Synonyms make our language more efficient, precise, and interesting. You know these synonyms:

candid	= frank	**scarcity**	= lack
query	= question	**requisite**	= necessary
futile	= useless	**dilate**	= widen
modify	= change	**lethargy**	= sluggishness

The more synonyms you know, the better and faster you'll understand what you read.

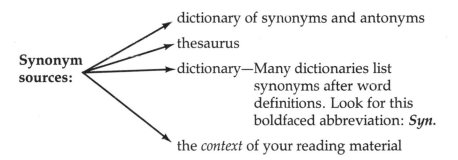

Synonym sources:
- dictionary of synonyms and antonyms
- thesaurus
- dictionary—Many dictionaries list synonyms after word definitions. Look for this boldfaced abbreviation: *Syn.*
- the *context* of your reading material

Context is the handiest source of synonyms for your everyday reading purposes. You can often find synonyms right within the context of the material you're reading. Words or phrases surrounding the words you're not familiar with can point to—or give cues to their meanings—as you'll find in the exercise below.

Your Turn! Ricardo was reading START SAVINGS BANK'S customer service handbook during his training for a telephone service position. He wasn't sure of the meanings of several words: "indispensable," "sole," and "effective."

Please see if you can help him, by looking for and recording cue words and then the meanings of these words.

SYNONYMS (Continued)

Good customer relations are an **indispensable** part of any service-oriented organization. Keeping our customers satisfied is absolutely necessary to remaining a strong competitor in the financial industry.

Cue Word(s): _____

"Indispensable" probably means _____.

_____

Make every single caller feel we are here for the sole purpose of helping him or her. Regardless of the number of incoming calls, focus your attention only on that person.

Cue Word(s): _____

"Sole" probably means _____.

_____

Customer satisfaction cannot be maintained without effective handling of customer complaints. The proper handling of customer complaints can not only keep a customer from going to a competitor, but in many cases can lead to additional business.

Cue Word(s): _____

"Effective" probably means _____.

_____

ANTONYMS

You remember that:

Antonyms = words that have **opposite** meanings

You recognize these words as being **opposites** or **antonyms**:

separate—join		erratic	—regular
succeed —fail		revenue	—expense
help —hinder		eagerness—reluctance
specific —general		tentative —certain

Your Turn! **1.** Can you identify the antonyms in this memo sent to an employee whose performance was unpredictable?

LOOK FOR ANTONYMS

> Some days you're responsible, others irresponsible. At times your reports are accurate; more often they're careless. Once judicious in handling your inventory, you now make foolish decisions. I've known you to be industrious, but lately you're lethargic. I hired you to be an asset to this department, but you're quickly becoming a liability. Do you want to be employed or unemployed?

ANSWERS: responsible—irresponsible; accurate—careless; judicious—foolish; industrious—lethargic; asset—liability; employed—unemployed

If you identified the above word pairs, you probably understand how antonyms work. Just as the *similarities* of words in a particular context can help you find *synonyms* and determine their meanings, you've just seen how *contrasts* in a context can help you recognize *antonyms* and figure out what they mean.

ANTONYMS (Continued)

Your Turn!

2. Use: a) a dictionary of synonyms and antonyms
     b) a thesaurus
     c) your own knowledge

to find an antonym (opposite) for each of these words. See if you can complete the activity in five minutes.

1. hire—
2. tact—
3. proficient—
4. germane—
5. delete—
6. affluent—
7. negate—
8. impulsive—
9. equitable—
10. peripheral—

11. superficial—
12. resolute—
13. obscure—
14. detrimental—
15. tedious—
16. benign—
17. impromptu—
18. parochial—
19. supple—
20. novice—

HOMOPHONES

- Julie began a long **ascent** to Payroll to get the **assent** of the controller for the purchase.

- Don't **shoot** agents' mail down the **chute**.

- The president **raised** the question whether the obsolete warehouse should be **razed**.

- The supervisor tried to **elicit** from the keyer a reason for the **illicit** transaction.

Note the four pairs of **boldfaced** words in the above sentences. If you can pronounce *either* word in each pair, you can pronounce the *other*, because *both sound exactly the same.* They are homophones.

Homophones = words that **sound alike** no matter how they're spelled

There are several hundred homophones and they pop up all over the place. Knowing the different meanings of each homophone in a pair *(sometimes they travel in three's or even four's)* will help you make sense of what you read.

Being alert to their **different spellings**—and using them correctly—will ensure that others understand your written communications, unlike the baffled nursing supervisor who received the following note from an assistant:

Mrs. Laval: 2:10
I have no more patience.
I'm leaving the ward.
                              Sue Duckett

Learn the spellings and meanings of these **homophones:**

- **aloud** = with the voice; orally
- **allowed** = permitted

- **board** = a flat piece of wood; a group of administrators
- **bored** = tired of a dull activity

- **billed** = charged
- **build** = construct

HOMOPHONES (Continued)

- **cite** = to summon to appear in court; to quote or refer to a passage
- **sight** = act of seeing
- **site** = place

- **close** = shut
- **clothes** = dress

- **complement** = something that completes
- **compliment** = expression of courtesy

- **descent** = downward motion; ancestry
- **dissent** = disagreement

- **lean** = to bend the body or rely on another
- **lien** = a claim on property as security against payment of a debt

- **naval** = related to ships, the navy
- **navel** = depression in the middle of the stomach from the umbilical cord

- **patience** = the quality of enduring difficulties with calmness; tolerance; understanding
- **patients** = persons under medical treatment

- **pore** = opening
- **pour** = cause liquid to flow

- **pride** = self-esteem
- **pried** = showed inquisitiveness; moved with a lever

- **principal** = a main person or thing
- **principle** = basic truth or rule of conduct

- **soar** = rise high
- **sore** = painful, tender

- **stationary** = not moving
- **stationery** = writing materials

- **their** = belonging to or done by them
- **there** = place
- **they're** = contraction of they are

- **threw** = tossed
- **through** = in one side and out the other

*NOTE: Don't confuse **through** with **thorough**, which means complete!*

- **vial** = bottle
- **vile** = wicked
- **viol** = musical (stringed) instrument

 Show your understanding of the meanings of the above homophones by inserting the correct words in these sentences.

1. The new drapes will _____ the conference room.

2. The future _____ of the firm's headquarters is still undetermined.

3. The _____ of racial equality will be fostered in this workplace at all times.

4. The lab technician will now _____ the serum into the _____.

5. Worker _____ over relocating was reducing the department's morale.

6. The sales assistants promptly ordered _____ new _____ from Office Supply.

7. The bank was forced to put a _____ on the company's new parking structure.

8. Each month I will _____ examples of employee innovation in the company newsletter.

9. Produce prices will _____ because of the Florida freeze.

10. He _____ the department $300 for the copy paper.

ANSWERS: 1. complement 2. site 3. principle 4. pour, vial 5. dissent 6. their stationery 7. lien 8. cite 9. soar 10. billed

HOMOGRAPHS

You know homographs. A 💧 (tear) isn't always a 💧 (tear); sometimes it's a 📄 (tear).

homographs = words that are **spelled the same** but **pronounced differently**—depending on the meaning the writer wants to convey

Some homographs are not at all related in meaning.

> **Example:** băss—the fish
> bāss—the lowest singing voice (or musical instrument)

(These often are one-syllable words and Anglo-Saxon in origin.)

Others are distant cousins. They have the same root but have taken different directions in meaning.

> **Example:** des´ert—dry, barren land
> desert´—abandon

The largest number of homographs have the same *basic* meaning but shifting accents (or syllable stresses) or changing vowel sounds—depending on their uses in a sentence as nouns, verbs, or adjectives.

> **Example:** The company received a **per´mit** (noun) to build a new waste management plant.
>
> The EPA (Environmental Protection Agency), however, will not **permit´** (verb) the use of polybenzalene in processing the waste.
>
> **Separāte** (verb) the batches by department. Store the **separate** (adjective) batches in the mailroom.

Please look up the following pairs of homographs in your dictionary. Insert accents and vowel marks. Write a sentence for each showing you understand its meaning. Notice that *the first one is done for you.*

dē´fect (noun)—Every time the team examined the completed carburetors, Alice found a defect.

dĕfect´ (verb)—Tony plans to defect from Cuba later this year.

HOMOGRAPHS EXERCISE

object (noun)—_____

object (verb)—_____

incense (noun)—_____

incense (verb)—_____

console (noun)—_____

console (verb)—_____

compress (noun)—_____

compress (verb)—_____

attribute (noun)—_____

attribute (verb)—_____

refuse (noun)—_____

refuse (verb)—_____

diffuse (adjective)—_____

diffuse (verb)—_____

deliberate (adjective)—_____

deliberate (verb)—_____

SKILL 22: EQUALIZERS

Multiple Meanings For the Same Word

As a productive worker, you've learned to manage your time well.

Becoming a more efficient reader requires *managing* the many words you meet in daily reading.

You can manage multiple word meanings by selecting—from a variety of possible definitions of the same word—the specific meaning the writer has intended. And *you can become good at it*

with

—practice

—a paperback dictionary kept handy, and

—an alertness to the **context,** or general subject matter you're dealing with.

Example: When you see "**resume,**" you may think "**begin again,**" (as in "The safety training session will **resume** promptly after lunch." But when you meet the same word in this classified ad,

> **Please forward your resume to:**
>
> **Manager—Human Resources Dept.**
>
> **PLATO PLASTIC PRODUCTS**
> **P.O. Box 324**
> **Pittsburg, PA 15219**
>
> **no later than Oct. 31.**

that meaning doesn't help much. It doesn't fit! In the ad, **resume** means **a history of your work experience.** *(If the French accent marks are present—résumé—the difference is easier to catch.)*

Your Turn! "Manage" the various meanings of the words on the next page by matching them with their meanings.

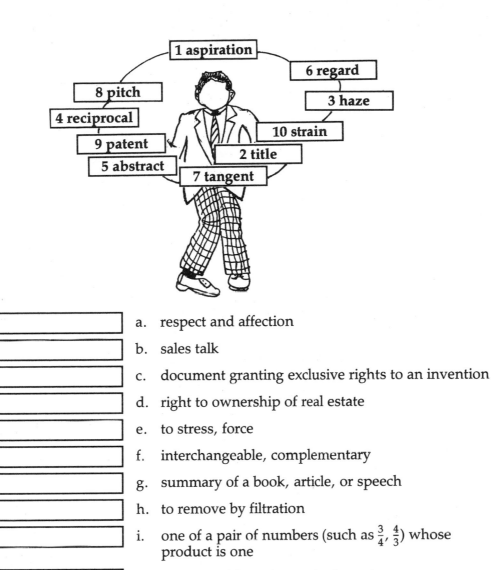

a. respect and affection

b. sales talk

c. document granting exclusive rights to an invention

d. right to ownership of real estate

e. to stress, force

f. interchangeable, complementary

g. summary of a book, article, or speech

h. to remove by filtration

i. one of a pair of numbers (such as $\frac{3}{4}$, $\frac{4}{3}$) whose product is one

j. removal of fluid from a body cavity

k. obvious, plain

l. abrupt change of course

m. to harass

n. sports championship

o. ancestry

p. opposite of concrete

q. desire for advancement or an honor

r. the degree of a slope or an incline

ANSWERS: a.6 b.8 c.9 d.2 e.10 f.4 g.5 h.10 i.4 j.1 k.9 l.7 m.3 n.2 o.10 p.5 q.1 r.8

APPENDIX

TAKING STOCK: INFORMAL READING INVENTORY

(Pronunciation, Comprehension, Vocabulary)

Please read the passage below silently and answer the questions that follow. Then ask a friend, co-worker, or reading assistant to listen to you read the passage. Underline any words you have trouble pronouncing.

---

*Workforce 2000

Major changes will take place in the workforce between now and the year 2000. Just like the population, the workforce will grow slowly. The pool of young workers entering the labor market will shrink. As the baby boom ages, the average age of the workforce will climb from 36 to 39.

Almost two-thirds of the new entrants into the workforce will be women. As their ranks swell, there will be increasing demands for day care, more time off from work, and flexible hours.

The number of non-whites joining the workforce will double. And two-thirds or more of immigrants of working age are likely to enter the labor market.

Manufacturing will be a much smaller share of the American economy than it is today. Its importance will diminish, much like agriculture's did at the beginning of this century. Service industries, like transportation, retailing, and health care, will create all the new jobs and most of the new wealth.

The new jobs in service industries will require much higher skill levels than the manufacturing jobs wiped out by new technologies. ''Unskilled labor'' will be a thing of the past. The fastest growing jobs will be in professional, technical, and sales fields. Very few new jobs will be created for those who can't read, follow directions, and use mathematics.

*Adapted from the study by the same name

LITERAL COMPREHENSION

1. Tell one way in which the workforce will change between now and the year 2000.

   _____

2. What percentage (or fraction) of new entrants into the workforce will be women?

   _____

TAKING STOCK (Continued)

3. Why will there be fewer workers entering the labor market between now and 2000?

   _____

4. Give an example of a service industry.

   _____

INTERPRETATION

5. Why may employers have to meet women's requests for more day care facilities, flexible hours, etc.?

   _____

6. Why may the U.S. have to invest more money in educating and training employees between now and the year 2000 than it had to previously?

   _____

7. Why shouldn't we be surprised at the decreasing role of manufacturing in the U.S. economy?

   _____

8. Tell why the information in this passage is important to you.

   _____

   _____

VOCABULARY

Read these words and tell what they mean, as used in the reading passage.

1. swell _____

2. diminish _____

3. economy _____

4. flexible _____

5. entrants _____

6. technologies _____

7. require _____

8. professional _____

9. immigrant _____

10. pool _____

TOTAL YOUR SCORE!

PRONUNCIATION —percentage of 219 words pronounced correctly: _____

COMPREHENSION—percentage of 8 questions answered correctly: _____

VOCABULARY —percentage of 10 words defined correctly: _____

See answers on the following page.

ANSWERS: <u>Comprehension</u>—1. There will be fewer young workers, more older workers. **2.** 66⅔ percent (2/3) **3.** slowdown in population growth. **4.** transportation, retailing, health care (education, banking, insurance, fast food, and other suitable responses) **5.** With the majority of new workers available being women, and these women needing child care, etc., in order to work, businesses that don't provide this help may be unable to fill jobs, or even survive. **6.** In the past, many manufacturing jobs didn't require a high level of formal education or skill training. New jobs in service industries, replacing manufacturing in numbers and importance, will demand much higher skill levels. To avoid permanently displacing potentially valuable but low-skilled workers from manufacturing, U.S. companies will have to educate them to meet the higher skill requirements of many service industry jobs. **7.** It's a predictable stage in the cycle of civilization/economic development. A country typically moves from a dominant dependence on agriculture (farming), then the production of material goods (manufacturing), and finally, the delivery of services—as its main means of survival and prosperity. **8.** any answer appropriate to the passage.

<u>Vocabulary</u>—(Any definitions that reflect accurately the ways the words were used in the passage are acceptable.) **1.** to increase, expand beyond normal or original numbers or size **2.** become gradually less, dwindle, taper **3.** prosperity or earnings **4.** not adhering to one, fixed schedule; able to be changed or adapted in response to special needs **5.** persons who enter **6.** applications of science; use of scientific, programmable equipment like computers to perform work or guide work processes **7.** need, demand **8.** one who performs certain specialized activities for a livelihood **9.** person who comes to live and work in a country that s/he was not born in **10.** a readily available supply

NOTES

NOTES

NOTES

NOTES

NOTES

NOTES